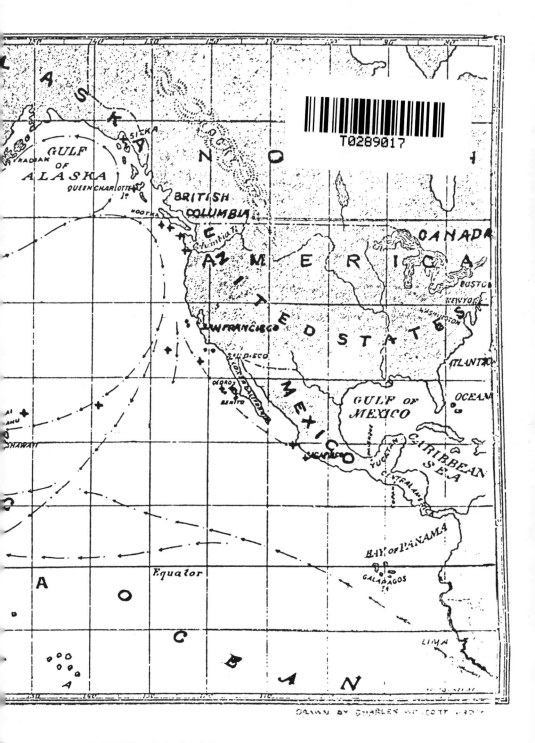

RTH PACIFIC OCEAN,

nts; also Direction of the Kuro Shiwo, or Japanese Warm Stream,
of Professor George Davidson, U. S. C. S.

ALASKA HISTORY NO. 36

A Japanese Glimpse at the Outside World 1839-1843

The Travels of Jirokichi in Hawaii, Siberia and Alaska

Adapted from a translation of <u>Bandan</u>

by
Katherine Plummer

Edited by
Richard A. Pierce

THE LIMESTONE PRESS

Kingston, Ontario : Fairbanks, Alaska

1991

U.S. Office:
The Limestone Press
c/o History Department
University of Alaska, Fairbanks
Fairbanks, Alaska 99775-0860

International Standard Book Number 0-919642-34-9

This publication is funded in part by the Alaska Humanities Forum, Anchorage, and the National Endowment for the Humanities.

Production: Pauline Higdon

Printed and bound in Canada by: Brown & Martin Limited
Kingston, Ontario

CONTENTS

Illustrations
   1. *Wreck and Rescue; Life on a Whaler*
   2. *The Sandwich (Hawaiian) Islands*
   3. *Petropavlovsk, Kamchatka*
   4. *Okhotsk*
   5. *Sitka (Novoarkhangel'sk)*
   6. *Return to Japan*

FOREWORD

Since time immemorial the waters of the North Pacific have circled endlessly, as if seeking egress. Passing the islands of Japan, part of the current splits off to go northward toward the Bering Sea, while the main current, named the Kuro Shiwo, or, as we call it, the Japan Current, then heads eastward toward Alaska and British Columbia. There part turns north to circle the Gulf of Alaska, while the greater body swings eastward and then southward along the west coast of Vancouver Island and the United States, following which, after lesser defections toward the Hawaiian Islands, and along the coast of Mexico, the main part flows south and southwest to the Equator, and after going west past Guam and Taiwan, swings up toward Japan, whence the whole cycle begins again.

For centuries, ships disabled off the east coast of Japan were borne helplessly by this current. In most cases the crews perished at sea, but from time to time a few survived the ordeal and were cast up on the shores of Kamchatka, the Aleutian Chain, southeastern Alaska, or even points farther south. Most of the hapless waifs were probably killed on sight by the local inhabitants. However, in some cases the shipwrecked men, enslaved or adopted, may have transmitted culture traits which in some degree modified those of their hosts. Archaeology may yet yield proof of such transmittals.

In more recent times, in more than seventy cases, shipwreck victims were cast up on land, or more frequently were picked up at sea by the ubiquitous American whaling vessels which in the 19th century combed the seas in search of their gigantic prey. However, returning the rescued men to their native land was then a problem, for Japan was closed to foreign shipping. Those who were brought back, somehow landed, in spite of the official prohibitions, were subjected to long and minute questioning as to what they had seen. Their accounts provide a valuable but so far little used source of information about the lands they saw. Katherine Plummer, an American resident in Japan, has done important work in studying and publishing their accounts. In this volume she brings the experiences of several sailors on the cargo vessel

Chojamaru, who drifted in the Pacific from November 1838 until they were rescued in March 1839 by the whaler, the James Loper. Subsequently they saw the Sandwich (Hawaiian) Islands, Petropavlovsk, Okhotsk, and Novoarkhangel'sk. Finally, by order of the Russian Imperial government, the men returned to Japan on a vessel of the Russian-American Company. They were interrogated for several years, providing detailed accounts of the several regions of the North Pacific that they had seen. One, in particular, Jirokichi, seems to have had a particularly remarkable, nearly photographic memory. His experiences were compiled in a book, Bandan , and the experiences of the entire group were placed in another work, Hyoryu Monogatari.

Survivors of other wrecks were similarly interrogated, and some of their accounts have been published, but the survivors of the Chojamaru brought back a particularly rich amount of information. The pictures made at their direction supplement their oral reports to provide a unique account of the life and cultures they observed, shedding light on tools, household utensils, dress and customs of the time. Only a selection could be provided here, and not in color. It is to be hoped that a Japanese edition of these important accounts will include the sketches and paintings in color.

Katherine Plummer, a teacher and author of numerous textbooks on the English language is a long-time resident of Japan. She grew up in Wisconsin and received a degree in education from Wisconsin State University-Oshkosh. A keen curiosity about early Japanese-American relations led her to study the Japanese language in order to read and find out hitherto unknown facts about the subject. Her interest has narrowed down in recent years to doing research and translating stories about hyoryumin (drifters after a shipwreck), these sailors being the first Japanese to reach America. In 1984 her translation of Funaosa Nikki (A Captain's Diary) was published by the Asiatic Society of Japan, and in the same year The Shogun's Reluctant Ambassadors, by Lotus Press Ltd. Miss Plummer makes her home in Tokyo.

Foreword

Miss Plummer's work on the Japanese drifters opens a new source of information on the lands bordering the North Pacific. If Jirokichi and other drifters provided their countrymen with a glimpse of the outside world, their testimony and accompanying sketches also provide posterity a century and a half later with a glimpse of the world that they saw.

Richard Kugler, of the New Bedford Whaling Museum, New Bedford, Massachusetts, and John Bockstoce kindly examined the sketches dealing with whaling and helped identify some of the scenes and equipment.

R.A. Pierce

INTRODUCTION

For the Japanese people living in the Edo period (1638-1868), when the government maintained a strict isolation policy, the world was about as narrow as that of the proverbial "frog in the well." No one, including fisherman and sailors, could overstep the coastal boundaries set up by the shogunate. Shorelines of every island were dotted with watch-towers and cannon to ward off foreigners. To keep the status quo and to discourage any interest in western thinking, the people were warned against any intermingling with foreigners or even disseminating news or information related to the outside world.

Considering this state of affairs one can imagine the excitement with which a group of scholars greeted four of their countrymen, never mind that they were lowly illiterate sailors, when they returned to Japan after visiting Hawaii, Siberia, and Alaska. What did the people look like? What did they eat? What did they wear? What did they think about Japan? What kinds of animals, trees and flowers did you see? What people did you like best? What kind of ships did they have? The curiosity and extent of the questioning can perhaps only be compared with the anticipation with which we earthlings would greet an extraterrestrial visitor to our planet.

Especially for the scholars of the day, who were starved for the intellectual stimulation and general knowledge that only contact with the rest of the world could bring, this event, in which men of their own flesh and blood returned after nearly four years abroad, was of monumental importance. Jirokichi, one of the four survivors of the shipwreck and drifting experience of the Chojamaru (1839-1843), was repeatedly questioned about every conceivable thing. Not only was he expected to tell the story of the wreck and the subsequent drifting and rescue, but he constantly had to jog his memory for intricate details of everything he had seen. Besides providing accurate descriptions, he was expected to make drawings of everything from the flora and fauna to portraits of prominent people he had met, and the scientific devices he had seen. In typical Japanese manner, the most minute details were not overlooked; descriptions extended to the exact size and weight of the teaspoons!

Fortunately for the scholars and government officials of his time, as well as historians of today, Jirokichi was an unusually astute observer who took an interest in everything around him. His natural talent as an artist enabled him to draw accurate illustrations, and besides this, he was endowed with a gift for picking up foreign languages. The latter was certainly no mean feat for a common sailor who had never learned to read or write in his own mother tongue. During his travels Jirokichi took advantage of every opportunity to learn all he could with an aim toward enlightening his countrymen in western science, culture and general livelihood. Consequently, Jirokichi's story, as told by Koga Kinichiro in Bandan (Stories of Barbaric Places), is considered the most valuable narrative among hyoryu monogatari (stories of sea-drifting).

You will not find the name "Jirokichi" in any Japanese encyclopedia or history book, nor the names of the other sea drifters whose fate it was to be carried away from their homeland. Some of them came home with fascinating and valuable descriptions of what they had seen in foreign lands. During the seclusion period these humble, unfortunate sailors were the only Japanese, outside of a select few officials who dealt with the tiny community of Chinese and Dutch traders in Nagasaki, to have any contact with foreigners.[1] Because of the rigid hierarchic class structure of the feudal period, a commoner, no matter how exemplary the deeds or services he may have performed for his country, had no chance for notoriety. Furthermore, as the drifters' stories were concerned with foreign countries they could not be passed along to the masses.

The phenomenon of drifting was not uncommon in the annals of Japanese maritime history, in fact, the Japanese language has a special word for it---hyoryu---sea drifting after a shipwreck. No one can estimate how many seamen simply disappeared after encountering heavy seas off the east coast, an area known as one of the most treacherous sea lanes in the world. In a few cases they drifted to off-shore islands, and many times the castaways were picked up by foreign ships. During the "Golden Age of Whaling" in the mid-19th century, hundreds of western ships, most of which were Americans, were plying the waterways in the vicinity of Japan looking for whales. It was these whaling ships which usually picked up Japanese drifters.[2]

How can we explain the frequency of these drifting accidents? As already stated, the busy coastal waters of Japan were exceedingly unstable, especially during the typhoon season. The peculiarity of winter winds also contributed to sea disasters, for the strong north and northwest winds would continue to blow up to ten days at a time. If a ship were caught in a storm followed by these sustaining winds, it would be blown so far out to sea that it would be impossible to get back.

Needless to say, sailors of the time were not instructed in the arts of navigation or meteorology, so once beyond the sight of land they were totally disoriented and had to resign themselves to drifting at the whims of the wind and currents.

The Japanese cargo ships of the Edo period were cumbersome arks that were convenient for carrying large cargoes on the inland waterways of the country, but their exceedingly high sterns made it impossible to maneuver them on the high seas. Shipwrecks usually followed the same pattern, that is, on encountering a heavy gale, the rudder that jutted out far astern would be the first to break. Then the one heavy mast had to be cut down to stabilize the ship, and finally the crew would have to jettison the cargo in order to lessen the force of the wind. Because the hull on the old-style cargo ship was sturdily built, the crew could sometimes drift for long periods of time. Of course the food and water supply was a contributing factor in whether the sailors could survive the ordeal or not. There were cases in which Japanese sailors drifted for as long as 14 or even 18 months, enabling them to reach the west coast of America.[3]

The strict edicts issued from time to time by the shogunate government banning any intercourse between

Japanese and foreigners applied as well to these seamen who were carried away from their homeland by an act of God as well as to all other citizens. Any association with a foreigner was regarded as a capital offense. So even when sea drifters were facing certain death they sometimes hesitated to accept the rescue offers of foreigners, but usually the pangs of thirst and starvation overcame their fears and they gave in to the bid to board the foreign ship.

Once the castaways were restored to good health they usually joined in the routine operations on the ship. If the rescued party consisted of several men, they were often parceled out among different ships. In many cases the Japanese were taken to the Sandwich Islands, a popular rendezvous for western whalers. The homing instinct, being particularly strong among the Japanese, always made the drifters long for home. Even though fully cognizant of the punishment they feared would be meted out to them, they were undaunted in their determination to return to their homeland. Foreign seamen, especially the Russians and the Americans, knew very well that the shores of every island of Japan were heavily fortified, and any attempt to approach a Japanese port would be immediately turned back by a volley of cannon fire. The only crack in the closed doors was through the port of Nagasaki and that applied to just a few isolated cases.[4] About the only resource open to rescuers who wished to carry out their charges' pleas to be repatriated, was to put them on a Russian ship that would take them as far as the closest Russian island to Japanese territory, namely Urup, adjacent to Etorofu, north of Hokkaido. From there the returnees could sometimes make their way in a baidarka along the Kurile Island chain, which came to be known as the "stepping stones to Japan."[5]

The sea drifters who visited foreign places acted as "ambassadors" for they not only informed their rescuers of their mysterious homeland, but they proved to be an important source of knowledge for their own government. The interrogations they were subject to on their return sometimes dragged on for years. There were cases in which repatriated seamen were confined for the rest of their lives in Edo because they proved to be so valuable to their government, or possibly because the shogunate did not want the information about foreign places and people disseminated among the general populace.[6]

In the case of the return of the six survivors of the Chojamaru disaster, two of the sailors died during the three-year questioning period in Edo before they could reach their homeland. Government officials realized that Jirokichi was an unusually gifted observer, and after determining that he did not harbor any untoward designs in regard to heresy and treason, he was allowed to meet with literary and scientific scholars over an extended period of time so that a detailed record could be made of this rare and valuable experience. Thus Bandan came about. Another book was written about the same drifting event entitled Tokei Monogatari (Story of the Clock), using data from the official testimony of all of the survivors. The latter was so-named because the Chojamaru drifters were presented with a magnificent wall clock by the chief of the Russian-American Company when they were in Sitka, Alaska. The clock was presented to Lord Maeda Nariyasu of the Kaga Clan upon their return and he ordered Endo Takanori, a noted mathematician in Kanazawa, to write the story behind the wonderful gift.

It goes without saying that the drifters made errors in their reports on circumstances abroad. Not only the languages were a formidable obstacle to understanding, but from the narrow point of view of these lowly sailors from remote villages in Japan, everything they saw was unfathomable. In describing what they saw, they were apt to dwell on oddities and the curious aspects of life among the natives. Considering these factors we can appreciate all the more the intelligent and discerning reportage of Jirokichi. He not only described many complicated inventions but he even advanced in English enough to carry on conversations which enabled him to make valuable observations on foreigners' motives toward his home country. But even Jirokichi's descriptions are sometimes sketchy, and information is often given in bits and pieces. Scholars may be frustrated when he dismisses important occasions or descriptions with just a sentence or two. For instance, he barely mentions the audience they were granted with King Kamehameha III.

Introduction

Koga Kinichiro, who wrote under the pen name "Yutensei," had been a brilliant Confucian scholar in his youth, but later he developed into a progressive thinker for his time. Being a vassal of the shogunate he was limited in his pursuit of Western knowledge, for his government feared the fascination learning about foreign cultures brought with it. Confucianism, with its emphasis on loyalty, was the backbone of the spirit of the shogunate government. Nevertheless, Koga's curiosity about international affairs and scientific achievements could not be stifled. With this intense hunger for learning about things beyond the reach of ordinary Japanese of his day, it can be easily imagined how excited he must have been to receive the invitation from the government to write down Jirokichi's story.[7]

Koga's <u>Bandan</u> was hand copied several times, but like other drifting records, it was kept out of the reach of the general populace.[8] The few scholars who did get to read it, however, realized its value and importance as a rare and candid look at circumstances in the outside world. Kenji Kiyono, a famous anthropologist of the day, after reading <u>Bandan</u>, described Jirokichi as being intelligent and perceptive in seeking knowledge. He went so far as to say that this book far surpassed all other Edo drifting records.[9]

Jirokichi seemed to show a genuine interest in conditions in other countries and how they related to Japan. From his observations and conversations with Western people and their way of life, he realized the disadvantages of isolation. But, of course, given the state of affairs of the time, he was not allowed to give expression to such thoughts when he returned home.

Though he did not press his opinions on Jirokichi, Koga's ideas flowed abundantly and were made concrete through his writing of <u>Bandan</u>. He must have welcomed the opportunity to enlighten his countrymen to the advantages of observing and studying other cultures.

The information that Jirokichi could pass along to his interrogators and Mr. Koga came at a time when the shogunate government had little access to knowledge of foreign countries, but was starting to show a glimmer of interest. Jirokichi's talk about such far-reaching topics as the power balance between England and America, the motives behind Russia's expansion in the Far East, and the circumstances in the strategically located Sandwich Islands must have been of great interest to the Japanese government.

Other drifters before the Chojamaru incident had come back with reports on the Sandwich Islands. They were superficial and brief, however, and only served to fan the spark of interest shown by the shogunate. The first reference made to the Islands was in Kangai Ibun (Strange Tales of the Surrounding Seas) by Otsuki Gentaku written from the testimony of a sea-drifter named Tsudaiyu in 1804. Other references made to the Islands were made by Zenmatsu in his interrogations in 1807 and by the Echigo drifters to the Islands in 1836.

Jirokichi's listeners were given a favorable impression of foreigners, partly due no doubt to the kindnesses and hospitality shown the hapless sailors. This was in direct contrast to the Chinese-inspired notion of only "barbarians" inhabiting the outside world. Jirokichi's report also refuted the widely-held prejudice against Christians in Tokugawa Japan. One of the most valuable contributions made by the Japanese drifters who returned home was in dispelling the belief that Western people were little above cannibalistic beasts, an image that the shogunate was not above allowing to be circulated among the Japanese populace.

While Koga was interviewing Jirokichi in his home, other interested scholars sometimes joined them. As they sipped saki and listened to the fascinating stories these men were inspired to write poems about the sailor's revelations. A few of these tanka-style poems have been included at the head of the chapters.

This book is adapted from a translation I did of an edition of Bandan published in 1965 by Heibonsha Publishing Company of Tokyo. It was edited by Yamori Kazuhiko and Murogo Nobuo. This edition includes not only the original text of <u>Bandan</u>, transliterated into modern Japanese, but also passages from <u>Tokei Monogatari</u> as well.

After translating <u>Bandan</u> I did a great deal of rearranging of the material. Koga wrote the story of the <u>Chojamaru</u> sailors' experience from drifting to repatriation and then arranged descriptions of what they saw under chapter headings such as, geography, food, dress, ships, utensils, etc. I have taken the liberty of inserting the descriptions in appropriate places in the narrative. This presented some problems because Koga did not always identify the location and nationality of the observations. I have included all of Jirokichi's descriptions, but I used only selected parts of the editors' introduction, and the author's preface and notes while keeping in mind the interest of English readers. We cannot help but admit as we read this narrative that Jirokichi was a remarkable observer but like anyone else in similar circumstances he made mistakes. He sometimes confused the English and Russian languages. He could not discern English and Russian sounds accurately, or perhaps Koga could not interpret the strange names and unfamiliar English and Russian words. Their crude renditions are written in <u>katakana</u> (a Japanese syllabary system used to write foreign words) and I have tried to decipher as many as possible. Wherever I could not determine the correct English or Russian equivalent I have written it the way Jirokichi or Koga heard it and added "phonetic spelling."

In this book Japanese names are written with the family name first as is customary in Japan. I have kept to the old-style weights, measures and units of currency. A table giving the modern equivalents of measures is given following the introduction.

Unless otherwise noted, the illustrations are from <u>Nihon Shomin Seikatsu Shiryo Shusei</u> (A Collection of Historical Materials on Common People's Lives), Sanichi Shobo, 1968, Volume 5. Both the texts of <u>Bandan</u> and <u>Tokei Monogatari</u> are included in this book. The illustrations from <u>Bandan</u> were all drawn by Jirokichi. It is not certain who drew the illustrations for <u>Tokei Monogatari</u>.

Introduction

I owe special thanks to my friend, Morikawa Jun, for coming across the copy of <u>Bandan</u> in a secondhand book store in Tokyo one day. Knowing I had a keen interest in sea-drifters, he promptly purchased it for me. This book is a valuable addition to my collection and has provided the basis for this book.

To my patient and knowledgeable teacher, Oyama Yasuyo, I am especially indebted and grateful. We have spent many pleasant and sometime laborious hours deciphering the contents of <u>Bandan</u> in order to come up with a comprehensible text in English.

Measurements Used in This Book

<u>bu</u>	-	3.03 mm.
<u>sun</u>	-	3 cm.
<u>shaku</u>	-	30.3 cm. (about one foot)
<u>ken</u>	-	1.8 m.
<u>jo</u>	-	3 m.
<u>cho</u>	-	109 m.
<u>ri</u>*	-	3.9 km.
<u>go</u>	-	.18 liters
<u>momme</u>	-	3.75 grams
<u>sho</u>	-	1.8 liters
<u>kamme</u>	-	3.75 kg.
<u>to</u>	-	18 liters
<u>koku</u>	-	180.4 liters (dry measure)

*The nautical <u>ri</u>, however, was equal to 1.8 km. It is not sure which Jirokichi was referring to.

Chapter I

SHIPWRECK

Even now...
Thoughts of drifting towards certain death
Destroy my spirit.

The Chojamaru, a 650-koku cargo ship, left Toyama in western Japan on the 23rd day of the intercalary fourth month of Tempo 9 (1838).[1] Captain Heishiro, about 50 years of age, was given command of the ship by its owner Notoya Heiuemon of Toyama's Kodera-machi district. The crew of nine sailors consisted of the following:

Hachizaemon, aged 47
Hachizaemon, about 50
Tasaburo, aka Chojiro, over 40
Rokusaburo, aka Rokubei, 31
Shichizaemon, 23
Jirokichi, aka Eijiro, 26
Gosaburo, about 25
Kinzo, 18
Zenuemon, over 40[2]

The ship sailed out of Nishi Iwase port (in Toyama) to Osaka carrying 500 koku of rice. Arriving at the end of May, the safe arrival of the cargo was reported to the daimyo's representative and then the ship was loaded with cotton, sugar and various other commodities. This so-called o-mawaribin, a ship that sailed from place to place, then set sail for Echigo (present-day Niigata) in the middle of June.

The Chojamaru landed at Echigo's port on July 6 where the safe arrival was duly reported to Toginya, the agent there. On the 16th, they sailed north to Matsumae in Ezo (present-day Hokkaido) where they docked in mid-August. Here the crew stayed at the home of the forwarding agent for about a month.

During the stay in Matsumae, 50-year old Hachizaemon, the helmsmen, expressed a desire to leave the ship because he had misgivings about navigating the dangerous route through the Tsugaru Strait and down the east coast to Edo. In his stead, a 49-year old man named Kinroku, who claimed to be an experienced guide in sailing the eastern sea route, was hired.

At the end of September, the <u>Chojamaru</u> entered the port of Hakodate where 500 or 600 bags of <u>konbu</u> (kelp) were loaded on the ship, and it sailed for Iwate.[3]   On about October 10 they arrived at the port of Tanohama. The harbor was congested at the time and wind conditions were unfavorable, bringing about a mishap that caused a large sculling boat on the <u>Chojamaru</u> to be damaged. A carpenter was hired to repair the boat, making it necessary to extend their stay in Tanohama by over two weeks.

During their stay in this port town, a Buddhist priest of the Ikkoshu sect boarded the <u>Chojamaru</u> to offer prayers before the <u>butsudan</u> (altar) for a safe voyage. A Shinto priestess also came on board and prayed before the <u>kamidana</u> (Shinto altar). She warned the crew to be especially careful around the 23rd or 24th of November because she could foresee the possibility of some disaster striking at that time. Since the crew members were all adherents of the Ikkoshu sect they did not take her prediction seriously and only laughed at the foreboding. The invitation for her to come on board was just a common formality and had no real significance to the sailors. It was also the custom to have a lion dance performed on board ship as a kind of exorcism, but this was not done on the <u>Chojamaru</u>.[4]

At this time there were 30 bags of rice on board. At Tanohama 20 of these bags were exchanged for 100 salted tuna fish.

After just a two-day voyage, the <u>Chojamaru</u> landed at Toni in the fief of Sendai, where they were forced to wait out a storm for about two weeks. On about the 20th, a fire suddenly broke out on Benten Island for no apparent reason. The sculling boat on the <u>Chojamaru</u> was let down to aid in fighting the fire. Luckily the famous Benten Shrine did not burn, but the trees and grass around it were charred. This blaze came to be known as the "Benten Island Mystery Fire." Also just before sailing from this port the sailors and the proprietors of the inn where they stayed heard a bell pealing at around dawn. No one had ever heard the bell before. Both of these phenomena were looked upon as omens, and the Chojamaru crew was told to be especially careful. The sailors, however, were not especially concerned about it.

On the 23rd, the weather cleared up and a strong tail wind was blowing. The crews of the 30 or so ships in the harbor quickly made preparations to sail. Only Captain Heishiro took his time in settling his bill at the inn and preparing to set sail. Heishiro, who had been a patent medicine salesman, was not considered especially adept as a seaman. Local sailors urged him to sail while conditions were favorable, saying "All the other ships have left and are already far out to sea."

Finally at about 8 a.m. the Chojamaru set sail. The port was very deep and shaped like a bag, so it took a long time to reach the entrance of the harbor. At about 10 o'clock a strong west wind came up. This akanbo or "red wind," so-called because the surface of the water looked red when it blew, was known by sailors for driving vessels to the southern part of the land. The Chojamaru was carried over two ri out into the offing. The sailors grew concerned for they had heard that when this wind blew it was impossible to return to shore. While trying desperately to adjust the sail, the rope holding down both ends of the sail snapped and they lost control. The ship gradually drifted farther out to sea.[5]

In the afternoon the sailors decided to jettison some of the tuna fish and 100 koku of konbu to lessen the force of the wind, and the next day an additional 200 koku was thrown in the sea. At dawn on the 25th the silhouette of Mount Kinkazan looked as small as an inverted rice bowl, making the sailors realize how far they had drifted. By noon their last view of their homeland had disappeared.

Having given up hope of getting back to shore, the exhausted crew now put all their efforts to keeping afloat. To cut down the force of the wind they dragged two anchors and cut down the mast. After swinging the ax just two or three times the mast fell in the wake of the gale-force wind. The men labored day and night to keep the damaged craft afloat in spite of the icy wind and driving snow, taking only occasional breaks to sip some rice gruel. The feeling of distress was beyond description. Kinroku, the pilot, determined that the possibility of returning to the coast was out of the question and said, "We can only hope to drift to a foreign country to the southeast." Now they had no mast, so there was nothing they could do to direct their course, besides they were not sure if there really was a foreign country in that direction. The men could do nothing but lament their fate.

At about 9 a.m. on the 28th of November, the wind changed to the east and the sky cleared. As the sea calmed down the sailors felt encouraged and put up the boom in place of the mast and raised the sail. The anchors were pulled up and the men put all their efforts to steering the ship in a WNW direction where they assumed the shore was.

To make their struggle more burdensome the sailors realized that they were already running short of rice. Usually when sailing the east coast route sea captains made sure that there was an ample supply of rice just in case of an emergency. But Captain Heishiro showed poor judgment when he decided to wait until reaching Kobuchi to buy more rice because it was cheaper there. When they left Toni there was only a one-half bag of rice remaining. To make the meager supply go further they ate only rice gruel.

Since the 23rd the sailors had been working day and night and only slept for brief intervals in turns. On the 29th, rain mixed with snow began to fall again and a west wind came up. The anchors were dropped once more. The unpredictable wind changed again the next day to the east and again the men set their sights on getting back to land, but soon a violent west wind drove them seaward once again. The wind continued to shift in this manner until the sailors were completely confused about their location. There was no recourse but to consult the Shinto oracles.

On small slips of paper they wrote the various directions or distances from 10 to 1000 ri. These papers were placed on a tray and everyone raised their voices in prayer to the gods and Buddha. When the rosary tassel was lifted from the tray they looked at the paper that stuck to it. They believed that this paper would tell them their position and how far they were from land. Methods of divination varied on Japanese ships, but the Chojamaru men followed this procedure.

Thus they continued to drift. On the 17th of December at midnight a big storm came up. The rope attached to the anchor at the prow was about to break from rubbing against the gunwale, so Rokubei and Shichizaemon tried to attach pieces of cloth to the gunwale in order to lessen the friction. To keep from being thrown overboard by the gale, they clung to the rope, but suddenly a mammoth wave swept over them with terrible force causing them to roll over the deck all the way to the stern. The entire ship was inundated by the wave, carrying away the sculling boat as well as the rush mat that covered the hold. Everything was drenched now and all hope for surviving the long ordeal was lost.

Hachizaemon carried around the Buddhist picture scroll from the altar in the bosom of his kimono. Rokubei also wanted to pray to the image, so they took turns carrying the holy picture. There was nothing to do but leave their fate up to Buddha.[6]

As a result of the sudden flooding, about four shaku of water accumulated in the hold and the men were kept busy bailing it out. Now they thought that if they were not hit by another big wave they might be able to survive. But the next day the sea was stormy again and waves washed over the entire ship. Everything, including the clothes they were wearing, was soaked through so they wrapped oilskin raincoats around their bodies and tied them with ropes. The konbu had soaked up water and swelled. This added weight

increased the force of the wind, and even though they knew
that they would need the seaweed for sustenance, they also
realized that it would have to be thrown overboard in order
to keep the ship upright. The tubs of <u>konbu</u> were so heavy
that it was all but impossible for the exhausted men to lift
them until Captain Heishiro took out some pickled plums and
gave two to each man. This seemed to give them enough
strength to take on the task. They had thought of trying to
dry out the <u>konbu</u> but it had become packed so tightly that
they injured their hands in trying to remove it.

All but three tubs of <u>konbu</u> and fifteen tuna were
jettisoned. This safety measure meant they might face a
serious food shortage later. There was little rice remaining.

All the men cut their hair and raised their voices in
supplication to Kompira.[7] They felt that their prayers had
been answered when the weather began to improve. At times
they were hit by strong winds and snow but generally the
weather was more stable. The sky cleared and the sea calmed
down enabling the men to devote their time to repairing the
damaged ship.

The <u>Chojamaru</u> sailors thought that by now they were
probably near some foreign country. They had all but given
up hope of getting back to the coast of Japan. There was
nothing to do but entrust their fate to the wind and current.

The dwindling supply of rice was rationed so that each
man would get two <u>go</u> each day. Shredded <u>konbu</u> was added
to the rice gruel. The dried tuna was soaked in sea water and
beat with a pole until it was soft. This was added to the
mixture along with grated bonito. It was boiled in rain water
with a little sea water added.

Before long only three <u>sho</u> of rice was left. Everyone
became agitated at the prospect of starvation. It was felt that
this dreadful circumstance came about because of the poor
judgment of the captain. They grumbled together saying,
"Why did he sell rice in Tanohama? Why was it necessary to
buy the salted tuna? So now we have no rice to eat." Little
by little the supply ran out and finally what remained was

divided among the eleven people, each one getting three go. Rice gruel could not be made any more as each person kept his ration to himself. Some simply chewed on the uncooked grains. By January there was no rice left.

After New Year's (1839) the weather remained mild and it rarely rained. This meant a scarcity of drinking water, and thirst became their greatest problem. Sometimes the men would tie a rope around their waists and lower themselves into the ocean to soak in the water. Others would put their faces into a bucket of water being careful not to open their mouths. This would relieve the feeling of extreme dehydration somewhat. Such desperate measures were repeated day after day as they pondered the futility of trying to stay alive. The sailors even stopped praying to Kompira, and now only recited the Buddhist chant, "Namu Amida Butsu," over and over again. All muttered in unison expressions of certain death.

By the 20th of January the drinking water was all gone. They tried boiling sea water for they had heard that licking up the bubbles would relieve their thirst. They tasted even saltier than sea water, however. (They evidently misunderstood the method for distilling sea water.) In order to boil the water they burned pieces of the mast and deck.

Only one sho of miso (fermented bean paste) remained and this had been soaked with sea water when the big waves washed over the ship. Gosaburo gulped it down anyway and as a result became so weak he could no longer stand up. In the night of the 24th or 25th when everyone was sleeping, Gosaburo stopped breathing. The next morning they all recited Buddhist prayers over the dead body and as previously arranged they lowered the corpse into the sea while waving the o-harai (Shinto wand) over the watery grave.

After a long dry spell it finally rained on the 26th. The men were so happy they ran around drinking as much as they could. Water was saved in every possible container. This was carefully rationed out each day. Even though mice and insects would accumulate in the tubs the sailors drank it anyway.

February was as warm as April was in their hometown. If a southwest wind blew they would sometimes get rain, but when the wind blew from the southeast rain never fell. They thought they must have drifted to the southeast of Japan.

Sea water was beginning to seep in through the nail holes where the nails had become rusty. Every day 40 or 50 two-<u>sho</u> tubs had to be pumped out. The men, who were by now reduced to only skin and bones, could barely muster the strength to perform the task of bailing it out. They would first stretch their limbs to relax and then stand up and set to work.

Shell fish were found attached to the ship's hull but they were not edible. They did find some algae that could be eaten which was growing on the wood. Seaweed sometimes could be found floating on the water; this was scooped up with a pole and eaten raw. They attached a bent nail to the end of the pole and succeeded in catching a few fish which they also ate raw.

One day a six-<u>shaku</u> turtle came up to the surface of the water. It continued to swim around the ship for several days. They thought it was surely a manifestation of the gods and Buddha. They tried many ways to catch it but the effort was in vain. A shark approached the wreck one day but they were unable to snare that, either.

Mid-April brought a broiling hot sun day after day. Rain brought relief only once or twice a month. Thunder sometimes rumbled but it passed over without bringing a storm. On April 20, just about a year since they set sail from their home port, Zenuemon died. He was given the same kind of sea burial as Gosaburo.

At times the sailors would chide Kinroku saying, "You said we could rely on you to guide us safely along the eastern sea route. Then we were driven off course and we have consequently been subjected to this horrible ordeal." Some showed their anger in rebuking the so-called expert navigator. He walked around with a worried expression on his face. On April 3rd or 4th Kinroku called Kinzo to his bedside and said, "For 20 years I navigated the eastern sea route and not once did I make a mistake. The sailors are saying that since this shipwreck happened it is proof that my time to die has come. If I remain among the living, the rest of you will not be saved. I feel that if my fate is terminated soon, you may be rescued. But I beg of you, before leaving this world I must have a drink of water. Please let me have my four-day ration so I can satisfy my thirst before I die."

Kinzo could not promise Kinroku he could carry out his request. He tried to persuade the navigator that the disaster was not his fault. The next day Kinroku again called for Kinzo to come.

"Please help me get up to the yakura [bow]," he said.

Kinzo repeatedly tried to talk him out of taking his own life, but he kept on begging for help. Kinroku could not stand on his feet alone so Kinzo put his arm around his waist as they made their way to the yakura. Then he earnestly begged for the water.

Kinzo went to the other men and told them about Kinroku's plea, but he got no sympathy from them. "That's a lie. He only wants to drink the water. It's a trick. Don't pay any attention to him," they said. But Kinzo could not ignore Kinroku's situation.

He went to him again and Kinroku moaned, "At least let me drink three-day's ration of water. Then I will die without regret. If that can't be done---well, it just can't be helped, I guess."

Kinzo couldn't bear to see him in such agony and again approached the others. "Please let him drink the water. If that man's words are a lie, I will compensate by giving up my ration of water," he pleaded.

The others mumbled together and finally gave in, "If you say that, I guess it is better to let him have it." Kinzo put nine portions of water in a tea cup and went up to the yakura.

Kinroku had taken off all the <u>o-mamori</u> (talismans) he had on his body and threw them into the sea. While repeating Buddha's name he looked up to the sky, worshiped the sun, and faced in all four directions. When Kinzo brought him the water he put his hands together and said, "I have no words to express my gratitude to you. You are still young so somehow you can survive and succeed. Soon a rescue ship will come." He gulped down the water and jumped into the sea. Kinzo reached out to grab him but it was in vain. The ship drifted away and Kinroku's body disappeared among the waves. When the others were told about it, they felt even more depressed. "We are all in a miserable condition and will soon suffer the same fate as Kinroku," they muttered.

Chapter II

RESCUE

Living and working together
Coming to feel of the same flesh and blood.

Early one morning in March when Rokubei was relieving himself, suddenly something like a mountain or an island appeared in the distance to the north. Immediately he ran to tell the others about it. For the last three days Hachizaemon was so weak that he was resigned to die, so he slept apart from the other men, but upon hearing the news he felt so elated that he crawled out to look along with the others. Gradually the mass of white came nearer and they could make out the shape of a ship. They knew right away that it must be a foreign ship because it had three masts. One of the Japanese yelled, "Oh, we don't know anything about foreign people." Another said, "Even if they kill us, I want to be able to satisfy my thirst." For the three or four days prior to this, the supply of drinking water had completely run out and the men only waited for death.

Then it occurred to the Japanese that if the foreigners saw so many people on board the derelict ship they might not want to rescue them. So it was decided that three people should alternate standing guard while the others remained out of sight.

The big ship came within two <u>cho</u> of the <u>Chojamaru</u> at about 8 a.m. It went around the wreck once which seemed to indicate that they should abandon ship. Three men, Jirokichi, Rokubei and Tasaburo seemed to be able to summon up more courage than the others and went up to the prow and waved clothes eagerly as a signal, and presently the ship stopped.

Right after it came to a halt, five or six men disembarked from the foreign ship and got in two boats and rowed up to the wreck. At this time those men on the

Chojamaru who were in hiding couldn't help but come out and see what was going on. All seven put their hands together and bowed. The foreigners in the boats then boarded the wreck. The men were dressed in tight-sleeved jackets, close-fitting pants and they all wore caps and leather boots. They observed the situation and the weak state of the survivors and with gestures indicated that they should get in the boats. The Japanese were so weak that they could hardly stand up but they wanted to put on their best clothes that had been put away. Captain Heishiro wore his silk crested kimono which the foreigners helped him put on. Finally they were all transferred to the two boats. The foreign men continued to inspect the tools, equipment, etc. on the Chojamaru.

Well, the seven Japanese were rowed up to the mother ship, a rope ladder was let down, and they were told to climb up onto the ship. Because of their weakened condition, a rope was tied around their hips and they were pushed from behind and pulled from above until they could get on board.

After a short time had elapsed the seven Japanese were taken to the captain's cabin. To get there they had to go down a winding stairway that went round and round like a [conch] shell. The cabin was about two ken four bu square. (In Japan this room would be called a tomo no yakata, (stern "mansion" on a ship.) A folding table about four shaku five sun square and about three shaku high was set up in the room. On top of the table was spread a white cloth resembling figured satin. It hung about one shaku over the edges of the table. (This cloth was used after meals to pick up and wrap the leavings from meals, such as fish bones, etc.) On the table were glass bottles filled with two to of something like sake. Around the table were set up seven chairs for the Japanese. They were each given a one go glass and that liquid was divided among the seven of them. The captain gestured for them to drink. It was sweet and smelled good. When the emaciated men finished drinking it and put their glasses down they whispered to each other, "I wish I could have another." In a little while some shallow rice bowls [saucers?] were brought out with about a half go of rice on each one. Sugar was sprinkled on top. They were expected to eat it with spoons. After a short interval they were given some more on plates. From noon until evening they were allowed to eat rice three times. Thanks to this nourishment they could stand up and they soon regained strength in their bodies.

After visiting the captain's cabin the Japanese were taken up to the bridge and the captain pointed to the Chojamaru. He had brought with him a slender piece of wood. When he rubbed it against something, it ignited. Then he blew it out. The Japanese could not understand what he meant by this at all. They only nodded. The captain then sent a boat out to the Chojamaru and soon it went up in flames. Then they realized what the captain was trying to explain to them. He wanted to get their approval before setting fire to their ship. The splinters of wood that he used to make a fire were about two sun long. He split the pieces apart with his fingernails, rubbed them together, and fire was made. (The Japanese had never seen matches before.)

The Japanese ship was burned because of the danger of it becoming an obstacle to other ships in the night, the drifters heard later. Among the equipment left on the ship, only one sail, an anchor, the pole used to raise the sail and a broken tansu (chest) were brought back by the foreign sailors. Other useless things like broken ropes, sails, etc. were burned with the ship. The kariorai (ship's navigation license) and a few coins were saved. The latter were divided among the crew by Captain Heishiro and kept until returning home. (About two months later he presented a short sword which was valued at about one ryo to the foreign captain.) When evening came the burning Chojamaru could still be seen on the horizon.

The Japanese fixed the date of their rescue as March 24, 1839. (According to the rescue ship's log it was the 6th of June by the western calendar.)[1] The Japanese later found out that the name of the ship was the James Loper, a 348-ton whaling ship out of Nantucket which they were told was a small island near Boston in eastern America. Jirokichi rendered the captain's name as Kesuka (Cathcart), a man they heard was of great wealth, having in his possession a fleet of seven big ships.

The drifters said that the ship was really wonderful. Its capacity was from 3000 to 4000 <u>koku</u> and it had a length of from 24 to 25 <u>ken</u> and it was from seven to eight <u>ken</u> wide. There were about 30 men in the crew, including a carpenter, blacksmith and a cooper. If any part of the ship was damaged, it could be repaired right away. The ship was armed with four or five small cannons with 500 to 600 <u>momme</u> projectiles. There were also four big cannons.

At the time when the <u>Chojamaru</u> was burned another foreign ship came near and flag signals were exchanged. This was also an American ship, the <u>Wabemecho</u> (phonetic spelling based on Jirokichi's rendition). Jirokichi forgot the captain's name.[2] Whenever foreign ships met at sea signals were immediately given. Whatever country they were from or whatever kind of ship it was, they always identified themselves in this way. After signaling, the other ship went around the <u>James Loper</u> and a boat was let down. The captain of the other ship came on board and talked with Captain Cathcart. What they discussed the Japanese did not know but they assumed the other captain was concerned about the burning ship. Later that night the ship sailed away and disappeared in the distance.

The seven castaways were shown to a cabin at the stern where they slept with the foreign sailors. The Japanese were so happy to have been rescued that they could not sleep, so they talked together all night.

From the following day the Japanese were each given four or five half <u>go</u> cups of rice gruel three times a day, morning, noon and night. Besides that, something that they thought was made from barley was given to them on a silver plate (bread?). They were permitted to have as much as they wanted of that. After seven or eight days passed they ate the same food as that served at the captain's table---rice gruel, bread, salted beef, boiled pork, etc. Sometimes fresh chicken and potatoes were served.

A few days after the rescue the Japanese were shown a big tub about three <u>shaku</u> in diameter which was about 7/10 filled with water. They were told to bathe in this. A sailor gave them some oily substance like pomade (soap) and told them to smear it all over their bodies. Bubbles came up and it took the dirt off well. When they put their faces in the water their eyes smarted, so they were told to close their eyes when they bathed. After the bath the seven men were given cotton tight-sleeved jackets, pants, boots, socks and caps to wear, so after that they dressed like foreigners. At this time Captain Heishiro presented his silk padded kimono to the foreign captain.

That night they were shown to a partitioned-off place amidships to sleep. It was like a cupboard with two or three shelves. Each space was about two shaku, four or five sun high and about four shaku wide. The shelves were in tiers against the wall and had one shaku boards on the side to keep from falling out. There was a cotton quilt over one shaku thick spread over each shelf as well as a red and white blanket. They got under the quilt and slept.

On this ship the three senior officers seldom slept from evening to dawn. The sailors also alternated resting throughout the 24 hours day and night. The Japanese were not given any particular jobs, so they slept all night and took naps whenever they wanted to. Some foreign sailors once said to them, "If you do that, you are apt to get sick." They expressed the meaning by using gestures but the Japanese guessed what they meant. Then whenever they saw them napping the sailors would wake them and tell them to come over to where they were working.

After that the Japanese were told to turn the grindstone that sharpened the whaling tools, and other chores. One day some sailors took a lot of cotton cloth from a chest and gestured that they should make some clothes. Not knowing anything about how to make western-style clothing they didn't know whether to accept or refuse the proposition. They finally agreed to do it after examining the foreign clothing and copying the patterns. After that they wore the clothing themselves.

The James Loper had come to this part of the world to look for whales. Other whaling ships also frequented the area. Sometimes they would approach the James Loper. When the ships came to within about one cho of each other they slowed down and an officer would put a gadget (megaphone) to his mouth that would send his voice as far as the other ship and in this way they could carry on a conversation. If the ship moved away before they had finished talking, one of the ships would turn around and come back and the conversation continued, or the ships were stopped. Sometimes one of the captains would board the other ship and thus they could talk face to face.

For about two weeks after the rescue when other ships stopped to communicate with the James Loper, the Japanese realized the captains were discussing the possibility of repatriating them. One time Captain Cathcart pointed toward them and held up seven fingers and blew breath from his mouth. The Japanese could not understand anything he said except the word "Uraga." They thought he meant that in seven days they would arrive in Uraga and this cheered up the drifters temporarily.

One time Captain Cathcart came up to Captain Heishiro and his men and said something like, "If we were to take you back to your country, this would happen." He gestured cutting off his neck. The Japanese then realized that he would not attempt to repatriate them.

The drifters could not tell in what direction they were traveling but they had thought they were sailing toward Japan. Then the ship slowed down and changed direction so they were confused.

After a month or so passed they met some other whaling ships named the New Neuyorogu (New York?), New Kayauka (phonetic spelling), and the Newburg. At that time Captain Cathcart suggested they take custody of some of the Japanese castaways. Consequently the captain told Tasaburo (now called Chojiro) and Rokusaburo (also called Rokubei) to get on separate ships, and Hachizaemon and Shichizaemon should serve on another ship. Captain Heishiro, Jirokichi and Kinzo remained on the James Loper.[3]

The Japanese were surprised to see live animals on the foreign ship. Some were kept as pets and others were for food. The dog was no bigger than a Japanese cat but its tail was longer than that of an ordinary dog. It barked very sharply when it saw strangers or met up with the pigs. One time when the dog took sick the captain used a kind of squirt gun (syringe?) device to inject it with medicine. It soon recovered.

The pigs and chickens were free to run around on deck in the daytime but at night they were kept confined to their pens. If there was any delay in feeding the pigs, they would be apt to chew on anything in sight. Because of this, their front teeth were sometimes extracted with pincers.

To kill a pig, they grabbed it by one leg and then quickly stabbed it in the throat. It was cut open at the rear end and the innards were scooped out. Then they washed and wiped the inside. The innards could be eaten right away, but one had to wait a while before eating the flesh. If the pig was small, say the size of a puppy, it was barbecued on a spit like a duck. Before roasting a pig, the cavity was stuffed with vegetables and the opening was then sewed up. It was put into a big iron box (oven) about three shaku square for roasting. The walls of the box were over one sun thick. While the pig was roasting it was sometimes basted with oil. But much oil oozed from the pig's body and dripped into the pan. When the pig was completely roasted it was stood up on a big platter. Its mouth was forced open and a block of wood was put in it. It really looked alive.

After everyone had sat down to eat, the captain began to carve the pig using a big knife. The vegetable stuffing was scooped out and put in a big dish. Then the other men cut off as much meat as they wanted, sometimes adding salt or a special sauce. The Japanese thought it was delicious beyond description.[4]

There were two black men serving on the James Loper.[5] One was named Anthony. He was not a native of Africa but was a Portuguese. He was 19 years old and was 7 shaku 5 sun tall and weighed 14 or 15 kan. The nostrils in his nose were so big that a Japanese <u>ichimonsen</u> (a 1/10 <u>sen</u>-coin) could be slipped in without any difficulty. Besides being very big, Anthony was strong. He could pick up Kinzo, put him in the palm of his hand and twirl him around freely.

Anthony was usually gentle but one time five or six sailors began to quarrel and a big fight broke out. Finally they all ran away and no one could catch them. Captain Cathcart was called and he declared it had been Anthony's fault, consequently the black man was scolded and punished severely.

Even though Americans strictly forbade gambling aboard ship, some sailors had dice. They were like Japanese dice except the one-spot and the six-spot were always opposite. Sometimes the sailors played dice when they got bored.

One time Captain Heishiro showed the sailors a small pornographic picture he had with him. All of them yelled, "Give it to me! Give it to me!" He finally let them have it.

A foreign ship came near the <u>James Loper</u> one day but they did not signal in the customary way to show their nationality. The flags were raised on the <u>James Loper</u> but there was no answer from the other ship. Captain Cathcart became angry. He ordered three or four cannons to be loaded with ammunition. Then he had a boat let down and ordered some sailors to approach the ship to find out the circumstances.

It turned out that it was an English whaler. One of their harpoon boats had just been overturned by a whale and they were preoccupied with rescuing a man who was thrown into the sea. They apologized for having overlooked the signal. Captain Cathcart said to Jirokichi, "If they had been a little later, we would have fired." Sometimes if a ship did not respond to a signal, it was fired upon with cannons. In this case the Japanese thought Captain Cathcart showed real courage.

About four months (actually August 1) after getting on board the <u>James Loper</u> there was a solar eclipse. The

Americans had an instrument called a telescope to observe it.
It started at about 10 a.m. when the sun was high in the sky
and lasted for about seven minutes. (At that time they were
located at $181°5"$ W. longitude and $36°5"$ N. latitude.)

One day Captain Cathcart said to Jirokichi, "You
people are always thinking about your parents, wives and
children. You seem to be very lonely. Do you know how you
can meet your loved ones?" The captain held up his hand
mirror and turned it around to show Jirokichi the reverse
side. There were life-like pictures of a man and two ladies.
Even their complexions were very natural. Pointing at the
picture, he said, "This is my father, my mother and my wife."
As he turned the mirror around he felt as if he was with his
family.

At the stern of the ship there was a big rectangular-
shaped mirror about three shaku long and 2 shaku wide.
Every morning the sailors took turns standing before it
combing their hair.

The Japanese were told that ships in the west were
made of hofusa, in other words the nara tree or Japanese oak.
This wood did not rot if soaked with water.[6] In Japan cedar
wood is used but it soon rots in water. On a western-style
ship the keel is covered with copper to make it more durable
and so it can withstand damage.

The drifters once saw the method used for applying the
copper coating. First the cracks were filled with pitch and
also stuffed with unraveled rope fiber. Then again it was
covered with tar before pieces of copper, which were about
one bu thick, three shaku long and two shaku wide, were
attached with screws. They were not pounded in like nails
but driven in with screwdrivers so the copper would surely
stay in place.

Ships were constantly being painted. When the paint
was beginning to chip or wash away another coat was applied.
The paint was of various colors. From the gunwale down it
was black, then at the lower decks there were horizontal
white, chestnut brown or red stripes. There was a narrow

white border between colored stripes. The colors varied by nationality but all the ships' hulls were not painted just one color.

For the pulley they used a white hemp-palm rope; for the rope ladder and mast thicker ropes were used. In the core of the hemp-palm rope jute was put in. Black paint was applied to the outer surface of the hemp-palm rope so it could be easily distinguished from the others.[7]

A chain was used on the anchor. The links in the chain were four or five <u>sun</u> wide and oval-shaped. The center of each link was notched and string was tied around it. This was done to give it more leeway and strength when pulling up the anchor.

Sailcloth was softened hemp cloth, strong and fine-textured like <u>kokura</u> (duck) in Japan. The shape of the sails was the same for ships of all nationalities, that is, they were wide at the bottom and narrow at the top. They were made like this because the wind was stronger at the top and weaker below, thus the power was balanced. Japanese sails are of an opposite shape and foreigners criticized them for that reason.

The rigging on the American ship was much more complicated than that on Japanese ships. A Japanese sailor could learn sailing in about six months but Americans said two years were required to master the art.

On the foreign ship extra sails were added or taken down on each side of the main sails according to whether the wind was strong or weak. The masts had five or six joints and could be raised or lowered according to how many sails were needed. When the sails were taken down they were rolled up over the boom and secured with ropes. All the sails were given special names so if someone called out the name of a certain sail, the crew knew without any delay where to go and how to carry out the order.

To stop the ship when there was a lateral wind the sails on the main mast were rolled up and the fore and aft sails were raised. If they did this, the wind filled these two sails and the fore and aft sections of the ship met the wind with equal force and the ship was brought to a halt. Western ships could run against the wind at a slant in this way. In a heavy rain, sails were rolled up to stop the ship from advancing and thus prevented the sails from getting soaked through. They didn't worry if the wind gradually became stronger but they feared sudden squalls very much.

Near the top of the main mast was a semi-circular watchtower (crow's nest). On the whaling ship it was about three shaku in diameter and about five shaku deep. It was made of slats two sun thick to which five-sun thick boards were nailed across. In the center there was a big opening where the mast went through. To prop up this platform, eight iron rods about three shaku long connected the mast with the platform. At one end of the rods an eight bu ring was set in. Around the circumference of the platform there were eight small holes in which the rods were inserted. From the top of the mast the end of the rope ladder passed through a ring and was tied. The lower end of the rods was about four bu thick and flattened. It was put through an iron ring and was screwed in securely. So the eight iron rods spread out like the ribs on a fan to hold up the turret. The space between the rods was narrow but both ends were somewhat separated. Around the edge of the platform was a raised edge about one sun wide and five sun high. On a warm day Jirokichi and his friends would follow the sailors up there and sleep while using the raised edge for a pillow and stretching out their legs toward the mast. Four people could sleep there comfortably. The ocean breezes helped them forget the heat.

Attached to the mast was an iron brace about three sun wide and seven or eight bu thick. At its end facing forward it forked in two branches several sun long. This was to hold the boom so the mast did not receive direct contact with it. The boom could move either way freely and at the same time the rope ladder was kept from wearing through. At both ends of the boom rings were attached through which small booms passed through. The space between the rings could be made wider or narrower according to the size of the sails. Pulleys were used to extend or lower the masts. Wherever the mast's base or rope ladder met with friction the place was wrapped in cowhide for protection.

As for the ship's rudder, the submerged part was covered with copper sheeting. The handle to operate the rudder was shorter than that on a Japanese ship and it was much easier to operate. The helmsman stood before a wheel-like device attached to the rudder shaft. There was a compass with a magnetic needle beside the wheel which the helmsman always kept his eye on. In the captain's cabin there were compasses installed in the ceiling and the floor so he could watch out for any errors made by the officer at the helm.

All countries' ships flew the national flag at the stern. It was made of sheerest silk and even though it stretched out to about one jo, when folded up it could be held in the palm of one's hand. At the end of the flag staff was a shiny wooden ball painted gold.

In the upper deck there were four holes. The two at mid-ship were one jo square. From the mast, the pulley rope was let down there and used for loading and unloading the ship. The forward and aft openings were four shaku square and were used for people to come and go. When seas became rough these four holes, as well as the cannon openings, were securely closed. Not a drop of water could get in. No matter how violent the storm was, there was no danger of the ship capsizing because of its size and construction. Below deck it became pitch dark during a storm, so many lanterns were hung from the ceiling for light.

There was no work to do at that time so the black men enjoyed themselves drinking alcohol, singing, playing the fiddle, clapping their hands and dancing. For this reason they sighed in disappointment if fair weather continued for a long time. This kind of attitude could never be imagined on Japanese ships.

At the bottom of the ship glass windows about one shaku square were installed. There were four or five windows spaced at intervals both on the port and starboard sides of the ship. Through the windows one could see the sea, but actually it was just a mass of green color. There were also holes spaced at intervals on each deck through which water was discarded. Also on each deck there were openings five sun square about five steps apart.

Upon arising each morning all the sailors cooperated in scrubbing the deck. They pumped up sea water to wash it off and then used fine sand to polish it. The iron cannons were also washed off with sea water. The high-quality iron was covered with pitch so they would not rust. Generally on board ship there was no distinction between white men's jobs and those of the black crew members. They all did the same work.

During the four months that Jirokichi's group was on the James Loper 14 or 15 whales were caught. Some were over 12 fathoms long. The Japanese found the techniques used on the American ship quite different from Japanese whaling methods. Jirokichi described them in detail. Standing guard for whale-sighting continued day and night. Two people watched from the crow's nest. There were lookouts from the top of the fore and aft masts as well.

There were seven species of whales. Among them the sperm whale had the most blubber. Since these were the ones from which they could make the most profit, the Americans searched for and tried to catch them. The sperm whale had a big head with a hole in the brow from which it spouted sea water. Its teeth resembled animal tusks. In its upper jaw there were no teeth only holes in the gum ridge which met with the biting teeth in the lower jaw. These teeth were used by the sailors in making various kinds of handicrafts.

The penis of a seven-fathom whale was about four shaku long. The skin was stripped off and this was spread over the back of the rope ladder and dried. Then it was used to make aprons. It was very durable material, they said. When the cooper manipulated a rusty wheel, they said, he wore this apron to protect his clothes.

Whales with a small head were called finbacks. They were very common and not valued so highly. The opening for spouting water was on the back of the head. Its teeth were like whiskers. Western people said there was little oil in this type of whale, so when they were sighted they didn't bother to pursue them. If they did catch one, they didn't take the wax from the head. They only kept the jaw bones. The meat of the whale was all thrown back in the sea. The Japanese thought it was a shocking waste. If they gathered up some off the water, the Americans would wave their hands and say something like, "That meat is poisonous. You shouldn't eat it." Or they would point at the bald head of one of the Japanese and say, "See what has happened to you because you eat too much fish?" Then everyone burst out laughing.

When the people in the crow's nest spotted a whale they shouted, "Thar she blo-o-o-ws!" repeatedly. Immediately upon hearing this the captain hung binoculars around his neck, pulled on his leather boots and climbed up the mast on the rope ladder. All the crew members could go up and down the rope ladder easily, but there were places where it was difficult to climb. When the captain got to the base of the watch-tower platform he had to pull himself up by grabbing on to the ridge of the lookout.

When the captain reached the crow's nest he used his binoculars to determine the species of whale. If he decided it was a sperm whale, there was great jubilation aboard ship and the ship ran in the direction of the whale. When it reached the proper place a chasing boat was let down by rope with two sailors in it. Then a rope ladder was dropped over the side and four more men climbed down to the boat, so a total of six men rowed up to the whale. As they rowed toward their prey, men on the mother ship signaled directions to them by using colored flags representing north, south, east and west.

In the chasing boat there were harpoons attached to long wax-coated lead ropes coiled in buckets. When they got within about six <u>shaku</u> of the beast one of the men threw the harpoon. The first throw was aimed at the head and this was quickly followed by another throw. If the harpooner was very skillful, he could make a direct hit at the whale's breast and the animal would immediately lose strength. If this was not done, the whale would be thrown into a terrible rage and it would swish its mammoth tail about and the boat would be overturned, throwing the catchers in the sea. Each whale was stuck with two or three harpoons.

Below the spearhead of the harpoon a long, strong rope was attached to the shaft. This rope was tied to the shaft by a separate cord. When the rope was pulled the attached cord was also pulled and when the chaser let go the grip, only the spearhead remained in the whale's flesh. The spearhead had a screw-like barb so it cut into the flesh and did not come out easily. The rope's length was about 200 fathoms, the whale would usually swim around about 100 fathoms trying to escape. After thrashing around for a while it used up its strength and then calmed down. The chasers would watch the situation carefully and then would begin to pull the rope in. When the beast had become completely quiet some men got on its back and thrust a long spear through its breast. Now the whale was killed.

As for cutting up the whale, first it was brought to mid-ship on the starboard side and a strong rope with a hook on the end was attached to the body of the beast. The other end of the rope was wound around wheels near the prow. It took about ten sailors to turn these wheels. As the rope was pulled the whale went round and round. A heavy metal chain wound around another wheel was used to pull the whale out of the water. When they did this, the tail always faced the prow so there was no danger of the ship being overturned.

Then from the gunwale a platform was let down on which two or three men stood holding a kind of sharp-edged spade. They proceeded to cut off the skin from the whale. First they peeled skin off the head, then dug a large cavity and scooped out the brains. Next the lower jaw was cut off and then the entire head was severed from the body. This was done by inserting a hook in it that was attached to a rope with which the men pulled it up on the deck.

The last thing they did while the whale was still in the water was to remove all the skin from the body. This was done by the men on the platform. As the beast was turned round and round the black skin was separated from the body with the sharp spades. While the body went round, the skin was peeled off just as if one were peeling an apple. Each strip was about three <u>shaku</u> wide, and the thickness of the white blubber was about five or six <u>sun</u>.

When the strips of blubber were hoisted up four or five <u>shaku</u> above the gunwale, they were dropped to the deck so that they crossed a double-edged sword. In this way it was first cut in large pieces. Later the blubber was cut into smaller pieces from five to six <u>sun</u> to one <u>shaku</u> four <u>bu</u> square. Some skillful people could cut it up into tiny one <u>bu</u> pieces. For this they used a sharp-edged tool with a handle on both ends just like the cleavers that the Japanese use to mince medicinal herbs.

These pieces were put into three iron pots placed at mid-ship where they were boiled. When they were boiling well, the skin and dregs were skimmed off and the melted oil was poured into a big pot through a strainer so only clear clean oil fell into the tub. There was a stopper at the bottom of the tub and when this was removed the oil fell into one of the five-<u>to</u> barrels stored below deck. Tie oil was perfectly clear and had no bad smell. It seemed to be ideal for cooking but the Americans did not use it for this purpose. The dregs were thrown into the stove. We were told that the refuse made excellent fuel. Because of this, whaling ships did not have to worry about loading a great amount of firewood for their voyages.

The inside of the whale's head was packed with oil, so a big hole was cut in the top of the head and the oil was ladled out and put in a barrel. It hardened in a short time and from this they obtained a high quality wax.

The Japanese were told that this had been a particularly lucky trip for the <u>James Loper</u>. Sailors were happy because their salaries were commensurate with the catch. One sailor said, "If we can sell our whale oil to an English ship going to London, we may each receive $500."[8]

In the middle of September there was a lull in the whaling operations and Captain Cathcart approached Jirokichi one day and explained, "If the wind is favorable, we will arrive at the port of Hilo in the Sandwich Islands tomorrow."

Jirokichi was puzzled by this. For over six months since they had been rescued they had been on a seemingly endless voyage on the vast ocean with not a single mountain in sight. How in the world did the captain know that they would be coming near land the next day?

Chapter III

ARRIVAL IN THE SANDWICH ISLANDS

Like bidding farewell to old friends,
We promised to meet again in heaven.

When the ship came within about two <u>ri</u> of the harbor the mast was raised and lowered all the way with signal flags attached. Seeing this two Cantonese merchants, accompanied by four natives of the islands, came out to greet the <u>James Loper</u> in a small boat.

The Cantonese were dressed in something resembling the <u>suo</u> (samurai ceremonial kimono), a white, wide-sleeved long coat. Over that they wore a thin crepe American-style tight-sleeved jacket. On their legs they wore loose pants. It was a hot day so they soon took off their jackets after they boarded the ship.[1]

The Chinese asked the Americans, "Where did these 'E-hon' [Nippon] [Japanese] come from?" The captain answered, "They were rescued while drifting." Then they said to Jirokichi's party, "Show us whatever papers you have." One of the Japanese took out from his pocket a sea route guidebook and showed it to them. One of the Chinese said, "I cannot read half of this." That is to say, he could not read the Japanese syllabary letters. They continued, "Where did your ship sail from?" Captain Heishiro wrote Nagasaki.' This they seemed to understand.[2]

While this conversation was going on, the Japanese noticed native men and women bathing in the sea; they then realized that they had come to a place with a warm climate.

The ship finally moved into the harbor, after about a half <u>ri</u> two crew members went up to the prow and from the port and starboard sides they let down a weight to determine the depth of the water. They found out it was about one fathom. The Americans were indeed well-prepared. In this way they knew it was safe to enter this harbor. Then the anchor was quietly dropped.

First the Chinese disembarked and then the Japanese left the ship with Captain Cathcart. Many islanders immediately gathered around the drifters and cried out in loud voices apparently grieving for them. The Japanese assumed it was their way of showing sympathy for their harsh experience at sea. While continuing to weep they led the Japanese to the home of a Chinese.

The house was surrounded by a fence. Within the compound were seven or eight thatched roof houses--some large and others mere huts. The latter were only three to five ken square. These were the quarters for the Kanaka servants. The owner's house was farthest back. It was about five ken wide and twice as deep. The roof was thatched and the door was western-style, opening on the side. The windows were made of glass.³

The Cantonese invited the three in Jirokichi's party to come in and indicated three chairs for them to sit on. He then congratulated them on having survived such a terrible ordeal. When the servants heard the story they shed tears.

The room was rather cramped but there were many wonderful furnishings such as dishes, glassware and other manufactured utensils. Also there were many books. The floor was not wood, instead there were grass mats about one shaku thick and on top of them was spread an anpera [rush mat].

Soon a fine meal was served. At that time the Cantonese did not use chopsticks. "In my native country, China, I ate with chopsticks but now that I am in this country I follow their customs," he said as he showed the Japanese how to use the knife and fork.

That night the three Japanese slept at the home of the Cantonese. They were given a large futon stuffed with bird feathers and a long pillow. Also he handed them a small box

only about three <u>sun</u> square. Upon opening it they realized it
was a sheer silk mosquito net. The Chinese man had a calico
curtain hanging over his bed.

Later that night the Cantonese called to the Japanese
from outside the mosquito net. Looking up they noticed that
he had brought some native women with him. He said,
"Gentlemen, don't you want a woman to hold tonight? The
captain suggested I bring them to you." The Japanese refused
saying, "We have been through so much suffering while
drifting, we have no passion left." They found out later that
the Cantonese kept several Kanaka concubines.

The next morning the Japanese found water in a black
lacquer bowl put out for them for bathing. Soap was also
provided. Again they were given a big meal. The drifters
asked the Chinese, "Why are you living in this lonely place?"
He answered," I came here not so long ago with the intention
of settling down here. I am building a home now." Then they
realized that this was just a temporary residence.

He had brought much cloth to the islands for trading.
Besides that, he was in the business of buying and selling
sugar and seemed to be making a profit from it. Also he
boasted, "Recently I bought a fine horse for 100 gold coins."
He took the Japanese to the stable and showed them the
splendid riding horse. Then he said, "Let's go sightseeing in
the area around here."

Hilo's port was on the northeast side of the island of
Owae [Hawaii]. The entrance to the harbor was over twenty
<u>cho</u> wide, on both sides rocks were piled up five or six <u>shaku</u>
high. A narrow sandy beach continued like a belt around the
inside of the harbor. In the coves they could see many turtles.
Further back from the beach grew sugar cane. There were
coconut trees and <u>suho</u> [koa] trees as well. The Chinese
trading company as well as the native settlement were located
near the beach.

There were three American churches in Hilo. The
Japanese were taken to the nearest one at the top of the
mountain. The minister and his wife were Americans. It was

the first experience for the Japanese to see an American woman and child. They thought the woman was pretty and gentle as well as being beautifully dressed. Her hair was reddish and they noted that the pupils of her eyes were almost white. The child was four or five years old and its hair had become completely white. Jirokichi and his friends were shocked by this. (Apparently the child's hair was blond.) The minister treated the visitors to watermelon, muskmelon and bananas (all grown on the island) showing hospitality to them while asking such questions as, "Are you going to stay here?" And generally trying to cheer them up.[4]

On the road going back they met six or seven sailors from the James Loper. Half of them were Kanakas native to this island. They insisted on Jirokichi and Kinzo going along with them to the red-light district. They had to push their way through thick sugar cane fields. To add to the difficulty, they had to avoid stepping on poisonous insects and lizards on the path. At one point they saw some twenty prostitutes taking a bath in the river. They thought it was strange that none of the girls had front teeth. When they asked the sailors why that was, they were told that their teeth were extracted soon after birth so they wouldn't steal and chew on the sugar cane.[5]

When they finally came out of the sugar cane fields the Japanese saw 14 or 15 low houses lined up, some big and some small. The first one was five or six ken deep and 2 ken wide. The roof was made of sugar cane stalks, miscanthus twigs and coconut palm. The walls were the same---not plastered. The building was partitioned off into six shaku square rooms. One prostitute lived in each one. There was a passageway down the center of the building and rush mats were hung over the entrances to the rooms.

The girls were sitting on chairs making knitted underwear. Between two partitions, a hole was dug for making a fire and an iron pot hung over it. It seemed that each girl cooked for herself. Since this was such a remote place, they didn't have many utensils. They used gourds for carrying water. When they were thirsty they simply held up these big receptacles and drank from them.

The girls in the first building said, "Well, let's enjoy ourselves," but the sailors said under their breath they didn't like their looks, so they left the building and proceeded to another building similar to the first one. The sailors were more satisfied with the looks of the girls there, so they decided to stay. They had brought brandy, cooked chicken and pork from the ship. Because this place was so far from the town, the customers brought their own liquor. The brandy was very strong so they diluted it with water. They brought only one bottle but it could be shared with many people. The sailors also brought fiddles, so the party became lively with everyone dancing, singing, eating and drinking.

The sailors suggested the Japanese pick out girls for themselves but just seeing their black faces and toothless smiles gave them a bad feeling. They refused and, begged to be allowed to leave before the sailors. The two Japanese made their way back through the sugar cane fields and again slept at the Chinaman's house.

Three days after their arrival in Hilo Captain Cathcart came to talk with the Japanese about the best way to return home. When he discussed it with the Chinaman, he said to the captain, "Japan is China's 'branch store' (the dependency-state idea). You brought them here to me and now I have no intention of letting them go." The captain told the Japanese in secret, "I think you can get home sooner by getting a ride on an American warship going to China but you must first go to Oahu. This is a backwoods port town. Only whaling ships anchor here. Since the Chinaman thinks like that, I'm afraid there is nothing for you to do but secretly flee from here."

Heeding the captain's advice, the three Japanese sneaked away from the Chinaman's home and again boarded the James Loper. Then, as one would expect, the Chinaman ordered some islanders to pursue them in a canoe. They came up to the side of the James Loper and shouted repeatedly, "Leave the Japanese here!" The captain yelled back, "God damn you! We rescued them and we will take care of them." But the Islanders didn't listen to him. The captain got more and more angry and was about to fire at them. The canoes finally turned around and went back.

The captain later explained the situation to the Japanese. "You don't know the circumstances very well. The Chinaman is kind on the surface, but there is hate in his mind. If you were to remain on this island, it is unlikely you would ever be killed, but on the other hand, they will make you work very hard and you will never be able to get back home."

The next day the James Loper sailed into the harbor of Lahaina on Maui Island. A sinker was let down to ascertain the depth of the water, the same as they had done at Hilo. After the anchor was dropped, the captain was the first to disembark. In the afternoon he came back to get the Japanese. Cathcart explained, "I went and talked to an American pastor named Baldwin about you. With his help, I think you can get to Oahu and from there perhaps you can board a ship going to China. I am quite sure a plan can be worked out to get you back home safely." He hesitated then and said to the drifters in farewell, "As for myself, I am getting old and..." He was choked with emotion and couldn't continue.

After offering their deepest thanks and fond farewells to the captain and crew of the James Loper, Captain Heishiro, Jirokichi and Kinzo got in a small boat and were taken on shore. From there they watched the ship leave for they knew not where. They stood there in silence for they had no words to express their deep feelings toward the ship and crew which had saved them.

The harbor at Lahaina faced south (actually west). North (actually east) of it rose a high mountain. [Puu Kukui-- 1764 meters]. From the coast the Japanese could see a path leading up the not so steep slope of the mountain. They thought that it may have been because of the flames of the volcano and the burning hot sun that nothing seemed to grow on the mountain.

The harbor entrance was about one ri wide, and like Hilo, rocks were piled up on both sides for breakwaters. On the banks beyond the sandy beach grew kao trees and coconut palms. A few native huts with grass roofs were interspersed here and there. In the town were beautiful homes built by the Americans and the Chinese alongside crude and small Islanders' huts.

Near the harbor Chinese traders were coming and going. One of them approached the Japanese and took them to his home. It was a fine tall building. The three men rested in a room on the upper floor where flowered rush mats were spread on the floor. At about 2 p.m. a Chinese official carrying a cane came to talk with them. They shook hands and then said, "We will arrange for you to return home." It seemed that Captain Cathcart had asked for the help of these Chinese because they knew about ships coming and going to Japan from China.

They stayed in this house for three or four days. They managed to converse with the Chinese by writing. Jirokichi wrote down their earnest plea for getting back home---"We drifted with a south wind. With your help we hope we can return to Japan." The Chinaman nodded. He wrote two Chinese characters meaning "Where from?" Then Jirokichi wrote "Japan Sea area" and showed it to him.

The Chinaman's next words left the Japanese completely crestfallen for he wrote something that meant they must stay at this place for at least three years before they would have an opportunity to go to Canton. Jirokichi's party doubted his sincerity when he added, "You are like brothers to me, so please feel free to stay at my place."

The three Japanese talked over the situation and decided to go to the American missionary's house that had been pointed out to them by Captain Cathcart. When they told him what the Cantonese had said he became very angry. Thereupon he asked them to accompany him back to the home of the Chinese. When he confronted him on the issue, the Chinese said, "That was only a joke," and he offered his apologies. The pastor gave him a good scolding and took the Japanese back to his home. After that they lived in the pastor's church.

During their stay there they had the opportunity to attend a religious service. The church was quite plain. There were no holy images or other decorations. The congregation sat on chairs in a large hall and listened while the pastor read from a book with horizontal writing. Each time the minister read, the people would repeat it. Later the congregation sang a song that had a pleasant melody. The service was rather long.

One day this missionary [Rev. Dwight Baldwin] inquired about the Japanese system of counting. They explained that hyaku meant 100, sen was 1000, ichiman was 10,000 and oku was 100,000,000. He smiled and said, "The Japanese system has few units." Then he added, "In America it is like this," and he wrote down many figures. Captain Heishiro could read a little, so he tried to explain about juman okudo [10,000,000,000,000] or the number of Buddhas between life and paradise [a great number]. He told the pastor about nayuta, which is the same as 1000 oku. It can be compared with gogasha [the number of grains of sand in the Ganges River, or an infinite number]. At this point the American yelled, "Suppiki Igirisu!" [You talk too much!] and laughed heartily. [Captain Heishiro thought he said, "You talk too much!" but what he really said was "Speak English!"][6]

After spending four or five days at Rev. Baldwin's place in Lahaina the three Japanese were put on a boat bound for Oahu. Even though it was a small craft, it traveled over the water at high speed.

Chapter IV

HONOLULU

Many people bow over the gravestone.
We cry for his soul in the lonely moonlight.

When the Japanese arrived at the port of Honolulu
they could see the King's palace on their right not far from
the bay where many small boats were docked. Cannons were
set up here and there close to the beach.[1]

In Oahu they were reunited with their shipmates who
had arrived in the Sandwich Islands before them. Tasaburo
[now called Chojiro] had come directly to Oahu, and
Hachizaemon and Shichizaemon did likewise on a separate
ship. Rokusaburo [also called Rokubei] first arrived in Maui
but later was brought to Oahu. Rokubei said that on his ship
piloted by Captain Jaeke, there were 35 or 36 men in the
crew. The ship was about the same size as the James Loper.
During the time that Rokubei was on the ship six whales were
caught, two of which were spotted by him.

One time Rokubei was involved in an accident aboard
ship when his head fell on a very sharp whaling tool. His cap
was cut and he was slightly injured. The captain applied
medicine. He scolded the sailors who handled the keen-edged
tool for being careless. Circumstances on the ship regarding
meals, dancing, etc. were similar to those on Cathcart's ship.

On Captain Poshita's ship, Wilmington, sailing out of
New Bedford, Tasaburo said there were 31 or 32 crew
members. He said everything was similar to the James Loper
on this ship, too. One time a sailor climbed up to a very high
boom. Tasaburo couldn't understand why, but the sailor
dropped down like a stone that had been thrown. He fell
with such force that one foot went through the deck boards.
He died instantly. This happened at about 8 a.m. and the
body lay there just as it fell until 4 p.m. Then the corpse was

wrapped in sailcloth and sewed up. A rock was put in it near the feet. Captain Poshita read some prayers and the body was thrown in the sea feet first.

Another time on this ship a waterspout caused a lot of excitement. Tasaburo went below deck and securely fastened the hatch. He felt the ship make a big lurch. When he returned to the deck and looked around he could see that the sails had been completely torn from the two booms. There was a very dark cloud about five or six ri in the distance.

While on this ship Tasaburo sighted two whales and a total of six whales were caught.

[As for the circumstances on the ship that Hachizaemon and Shichizaemon served on, they are not recorded.]

Three days after landing at Honolulu, Captain Jaeke took Rokubei to the home of a wealthy Cantonese dry goods merchant named Papiyu [phonetic spelling]. He found Hachizaemon and Shichizaemon already there. Tasaburo did not arrive until ten days later. When his ship arrived in Honolulu Captain Poshita first went to Papiyu's house. He couldn't understand what they were talking about, so he went back to the ship and got Tasaburo. Upon seeing the Chinaman's house, Tasaburo thought at first that it must be the King's residence. There was a big gate in front of the two-story stone mansion. Cannons were set up all around the building. When Tasaburo stepped on the verandah a woman who seemed to be the master's wife came out to greet him and showed him into a big room.

The interior of the house had wooden floors. In the middle of the living room was a big table. The woman sat facing the Japanese at the head of the table. Tasaburo was offered a chair and a kiseru [a long Japanese pipe with a small bowl] and tobacco. A candle was lit to prepare the pipe for smoking. Tea was offered, too. After some time had elapsed a meal was served.

The master and his wife were dark-complexioned.
Papiyu was especially fat, like a [sumo] wrestler.

Well, Jirokichi's party did not stay at the same place
when they arrived in Honolulu.   Through a letter of
introduction from Rev. Baldwin, they were put in the care of
a Mr. Beimon [Rev. Hiram Bingham]. Across the street from
his house was the home of a doctor named Kaoka [Dr. Gerrit
P. Judd]. Next to his home on the left was a printing plant.
The three Japanese were asked to stay with Dr. Judd.

They spent their time going sightseeing around
Honolulu and its environs.   Jirokichi later described the
circumstances to his questioners in his homeland.

The harbor of Honolulu opened toward the west.
Smoothly undulating mountains [the Kulua Range] surrounded
the city.   On the lower slopes sandalwood trees grew
luxuriantly.   It was always warm so trees laden with fruit
could be seen here and there.

Rocks were piled up for breakwaters on either side of
the harbor, the one on the left projected about 200 ken into
the sea and the other about 150 ken.   Between the
breakwaters, it was a distance of about two cho. The harbor
was rather shallow so big warships could not enter, instead
they anchored about   ri in the offing. Whaling ships could
enter, however. During the 10 or 15 day period from the end
of August to early September 70 or 80 ships entered the
harbor. The masts looked like a forest. On special occasions
and on Sundays when ships were docked at the harbor many
colored flags were hung from ropes strung from stem to stern.
When they all fluttered simultaneously in the wind it was
really a beautiful sight.

At the north end of the harbor there was a structure
made of big timbers in a T-shape formation. Boats came up
alongside this platform while loading and unloading cargo on
ships.   The part that was in the water was covered with
copper. The crosspiece on top was about five ken long and
three ken wide; the vertical sections were about three ken
long and 2 ken wide. It looked like a bridge.

The city of Honolulu was a bustling trading center with merchants from America, England, Luzon [the Philippines], Australia, Sumatra, and Bengal, besides the Chinese. There were no Russian traders.

The native Hawaiians always walked around barefoot like the Ainu in Japan. In the country they wore no clothes. The Japanese saw completely nude men and women working in the fields, some of the men having tattoos all over their bodies. Inside the home they wore a kind of loin cloth made of paper [tapa?] which was thick and strong like <u>shibugame</u> [a Japanese hand-made paper treated with astringent persimmon juice]. When they went to the city they wore clothing.

The natives, or Kanakas, in the city wore clothes made of cotton cloth. Jirokichi said that he heard from an old man that up until 22 or 23 years before the natives wore no clothes to speak of, only a few tree leaves. It was only after the arrival of the foreign settlers that they wrapped their bodies in cotton cloth.

Island women tied up their hair like it is done in Japan with a topknot and some hanging down on both sides. In the topknot they inserted a large coarse-toothed tortoise shell comb. For special occasions they added combs on both sides or a wreath of leaves. Their complexions were usually bad.

Jirokichi noted that like the prostitutes they had seen in Hilo, many islanders in Oahu had no front teeth. When he asked about it in this place he was told that according to ancient religious beliefs, Sandwich Islanders made a vow to their gods when entering the faith that they would have their two lower front teeth extracted. American missionaries strictly forbade the custom, so now it was not so commonly practiced.

The Americans and Englishmen dressed pretty much alike. Bengali men were similarly dressed but their skin and hair color was totally black. There were black people from America like those on the ship. The black people's hair was generally thin, kinky, dirty and full of dandruff. They liked to play the fiddle here, too. Placing the instrument under their chin, they raised their left hand to support it and used their fingers to press the strings while moving the bow with the right hand. It was much different from the way musical instruments were played in Japan.

There were also some people from South America called Irigini [?]. They walked around naked with their hair hanging down loosely, but they had majestic physiques.

The Japanese were told that there were no prostitutes in Honolulu, but some people said there were "secret prostitutes." Some had husbands who consented to the practice in order to supplement their incomes. The customers would come as "guests" to their homes. If the public found out about it, they would be censured, so the husband would stand out in front by the gate when the "guest" was there.

The Chinese traders who hailed from the Canton area were called pake by the Islanders, a word meaning "special guests." Some Islanders said to the Japanese, "Pake people tell many lies, they don't know much about anything." A Chinese, in turn, said about the Islanders, "Kanakas are robbers. One time they came into my shop and stole some brocade and fled into the mountains in their bare feet."

There were about 200 native dwellings in the city. They were small and shabby adobe huts with grass roofs. It didn't rain very much and there were no earthquakes so there was little danger of the crudely constructed huts collapsing.

By comparison, the Americans' homes were beautifully built of wood painted white both outside and inside. The slate or sheet metal roofs were somewhat curved like the Japanese Shinto style. A verandah surrounded the entire second floor where people would walk around or sit and enjoy the cool breeze. Glass doors and windows here and there opened out on the verandah. The floors were made of thick boards on which rugs or rush mats were spread. Foreign people do not take off their shoes when entering the house.

All the traders' shops looked pretty much alike. Big glass windows in front showed a display of merchandise. Two or three clerks inside were watching over the beautiful cloth and rugs. In the back of the shop more materials were kept in many chests of drawers. The companies accommodated their customers by providing benches in front of their establishments where they could enjoy the cool evening air.

The Japanese rode in a horse-drawn carriage one day. Besides the two wheels in the center, it had an extra wheel in front attached to the yoke. Well-forged layers of iron [springs] underneath expanded and contracted when going up or down slopes so it didn't shake, and passengers could ride along the road smoothly. Some of the carriages had roofs. They were drawn by three or four horses.

Every morning there was a flourishing open market in Honolulu held in an area three or four cho long and about one cho wide. Clothing, food and other daily necessities were sold there, as well as the staple food of the islands--poi. On Sundays everybody took a holiday. One time Jirokichi went in a Bengali shop owned by a man named Mamake [phonetic spelling]. He gave the Japanese some pieces of coral about three sun long. Jirokichi secretly sold one piece but saved the others to take home. The coral was not of very high quality as it had worm holes in it. The Bengali told Jirokichi that there was much coral in India.

In the neighborhood where the Japanese lived there were many "temples" [churches]. The Japanese noted, "If it were in Japan, it would be called a teramachi [temple town]. Rev. Bingham, who the Japanese guessed was about 55 or 56 years old [actually 50] at this time was one of the first American residents in the Sandwich Islands, having come to teach about Jesus Christ. At first the Kanakas would not accept Christianity at all, the Japanese were told. One time a knife-wielding native tried to kill the pastor. Now it was said that eight or nine people out of ten had been converted. The Christians were building a big church while the Japanese were there. They heard that seven years had already been spent on its construction and seven or eight more years would be needed to complete it.

Rev. Bingham showed Jirokichi some landscape paintings in which churches in America were depicted. In the church that was being constructed the ceiling was very high. The front of the building [steeple] was higher than the back. A big clock was set in the front which had a device that made the bells ring automatically on the hour.[2]

In Honolulu it was warm throughout the year. The temperature dropped a little at night, and in November and December people wore lined clothing. During the other months it was always about the same temperature as it is in June in Japan. Usually the sky was blue, but occasionally there were showers and sometimes thunderstorms. The length of day varied according to the season like in Japan.

The Sandwich Islands consisted of nine islands, according to Jirokichi. Among them, two were uninhabited. The royal palace was located on Oahu Island in Honolulu. The Islands were part of the British Empire [Jirokichi misunderstood this]. Religion and education were introduced by the Americans. There were ten times as many Americans as English people in the islands. King Kamehameha III was the king in name only, in truth, America had the authority.

English people ridiculed the king calling him the "Sugar King." Under the king there were administrative officials called alei. Each island was ruled by an alei whom their subjects called ken [king] as a title of respect. Their social status was high.

Among these ken there were women, too. Many of these women were giants. Some of them were so obese that they could not walk so they rode on a special cart when they went out. It was said that they ate ereo [dog] meat, some eating one a day. Sometimes the women would lie on their bellies and catch live fish with their hands, sprinkle salt on them, and eat them. The Japanese drifters thought such a vulgar custom was very strange.

Jirokichi heard that England was already in possession of 6/10 of the world. The English said that in another hundred years the whole world would be unified and be living under English customs. Also in "English America" each of the 24 states sent one representative to the national government. That office was like the Japanese soncho [town mayor]. Also for making inspection tours of each province they used a "manowa" [meaning a "man-o'-war ship--Jirokichi did not understand this]. The officials on the "manowa" had the authority of disciplining whaling captains, if any complaints were found to be legitimate the captains were punished directly by these officials. This "manowa" was sent out by the central government to oversee the ships.

Every country had man-o'-war ships that represented power. On the sea and on land they had inspection tours. When an English man-o'-war arrived at a busy port the sailors took off their caps and by using threats demanded that passersby fill the caps with money. [Jirokichi saw such plundering both in the Sandwich Islands and Okhotsk]. Russian officers said that they saw the English doing it in Irkutsk and Moscow, too. The English officers did indulge in greedy ways and every other country looked upon it with displeasure. Since England was so strong they could do nothing about it. [Koga adds that he cannot believe this story.]

The Japanese were honored with an audience with the king when they were staying in Honolulu.[3]   The palace grounds spread many tens of ken from north to south. The gate facing east was open. To the left of the gate the large flag given to the king by the English was flying. It had red and white horizontal stripes and was about three shaku long and five shaku wide.

Inside the gate was a big parade ground surrounded by a wall. The lower part of the wall was stone and above that was adobe about two ken thick and equally high. Here and there the earthen part stuck out and receded so the wall was not exactly square. There were several buildings within the compound.

The area around the palace was heavily fortified. Every few steps there was a big cannon mounted on a stand. The biggest ones were over one jo long with apertures one shaku in diameter. There were four or five of these huge bronze cannons. Beside them were innumerable projectiles piled up to look like a roofed hut. None of them seemed to be rusty from the dew or rain.

When they met the king the Japanese took off their caps and held them under their left arms and saluted western style. The king returned the salute and extended his arm to shake hands. He said, "Please come and visit me sometimes." In this way the Japanese thought he showed more deference toward foreigners than he did to his own subjects. Of course they were offered poi, but it tasted so sour that they kept their mouths clamped shut. But when watermelon was served they were happy.

It was not far from the front of the palace to the streets of the town. There were no gun platforms there but cannons were set up in the part of the city facing the sea in four places. North of the city there were ten cannons. Jirokichi was quite sure that they were mounted on stands with wheels but he couldn't remember clearly. Near the breakwater on the left there were also ten cannons. These were simply placed on the ground with no stands. Near the place where salt was manufactured 14 or 15 cannons were arranged in two tiers on a big rock. These cannons were about seven shaku long with apertures about four sun in diameter. The fourth cannon placement was south of the city where there were ten or more of the biggest cannons of all.

About a month after arriving in Honolulu Captain Heishiro became ill. He gradually became weaker and in spite of Dr. Judd's treatments, he breathed his last at the end of October. When Jirokichi ran to tell Rev. Bingham he went to report it to the governor. An official and his assistant came to examine the body. That night all the Japanese gathered for a wake.

Rev. Bingham arranged the funeral service. First the captain's remains were put in a wooden coffin. This was covered with a cloth and put on a wagon. A thick cotton cord was attached and native people pulled it. Rev. Bingham walked at the head of the procession holding a Bible that was about three <u>sun</u> thick. Other ministers followed, then the six Japanese sailors, and then many local people.

A grave seven or eight <u>shaku</u> deep had been dug next to some graves for Rev. Bingham's three children who had died one after the other the year before. The coffin was lowered into the grave while Rev. Bingham spoke and read prayers. The service lasted over three hours. Each attendee was asked to fill in the grave with a hoe. There were about 300 people so when the earth was all gone they merely made the gesture. That was the end.[4]

A thick board was set up to mark the grave. It was about four <u>shaku</u> high and one <u>shaku</u> wide. The front was painted white. The top was covered with a kind of triangular-shaped roof. Heishiro's sailors were asked to write on the board with some black asphalt-like implement something about Captain Heishiro's life and drifting experience. The drifters were troubled about it because none of them ever learned to read or write. Finally Jirokichi wrote a short epitaph in horizontal lines in <u>katakana</u>. It said:

Dai Nippon

Ecchu no kuni Toyama Kimachi ura jiki sendo
Yoshiokaya Heishiro gojusansai konotabi kono
tokoro ni ochikite, naganaga byoki ni tsuki,
kono tokoro nita byoshi ni oyobu.

Great Nippon

On a ship from Kimachi town in Toyama, Ecchu
province,
Captain Yoshiokaya Heishiro, 53, came to
this place. After a lengthy illness, died of
natural causes at this place.

Rev. Bingham translated Jirokichi's words and added a note: "Whenever a Japanese comes to this island in the future, we will give the details of the captain's death along with the proof." He said to the sailors, "When some building stone is brought from America a proper gravestone will be erected."[5]

Four or five days after the funeral the pastor planted four plants with red flowers in front of the captain's tombstone. A fence about eight shaku square and three shaku high was put up to protect the grave.

After the captain's death all of the Japanese were serving in the home of the Chinese merchant, Papiyu. Only Jirokichi remained at Dr. Judd's home. When he got lonely he would go over to Papiyu's place. One day Papiyu said to him, "I'm afraid that if you continue to stay in that house, you will die like Heishiro. How about coming here to live?" His shipmates encouraged Jirokichi too, so when he got back to the doctor's home he said to him, "I would like to have your permission to live with my friends." Dr. Judd replied, "If it is lonely for you here, you had better do that. If you are not comfortable there, however, please feel free to come back any time." So from that day, Jirokichi began to help in the home of the Chinese merchant, too.

One day Papiyu showed the Japanese one of his treasures. It was a black bowl coated with red lacquer with a few pickled plums in it. This had been given to him by some Japanese who had drifted to the Sandwich Islands in 1832. They were from Hayakawa village in Echigo province.[6]

The Chinese sometimes told the Japanese to change their hairstyle. The Chinese shaved their heads except for one braid that hung down the back. The sailors refused to comply with their request.

In Papiyu's home there were beautiful tansu [Oriental chests of drawers] with rows of shallow drawers on both sides. They were locked in the same way as the Japanese tsukiake style. The plate that was inserted was made from whale teeth. The Chinese also had clocks and watches in his home. There were two or three clocks in some homes. Even horse drivers carried pocket watches.

They used lanterns with isinglass on iron frames. They were various shapes---some five-sided, six-sided or eight-sided. The lantern could rotate as it hung from a ring attached to a finial. The isinglass was pliable but it didn't break. The top of the lantern was open to let air in. To prevent the candle inside from toppling over, it was set in a pipe base. Inside of that the candle was wound on a screw. There was a spring made of gold wire to support the lower end of the candle which pushed the candle up as it burned thus enabling it to last as long as possible. There was a plate under the pipe where the drippings fell.

The Americans and the English used only gold and silver coins, they had no paper money. In the Sandwich Islands Peruvian gold coins were prevalent, so Jirokichi assumed that must be a rich country. Their coins were round and flat with a two-winged horse engraved on them. Chinese people carved the ideograph [king] on American silver coins and sent them to China where they were put in circulation. The Japanese were told that they had the approval of the Chinese emperor to do that.

Among the many kinds of tropical trees that grew in the sandy soil on the island was the coconut. The Japanese sometimes picked and ate the fruit. Where the branches of the tree had dropped off stumps were left that served as footholds enabling them to climb the trees. When the coconuts were still unripe they were full of a sweet but slightly astringent juice, something like amazaka [sweet sak] in Japan. When the fruit became ripe the flesh inside the shell was very sweet, but there was no juice. This fleshy part was about five bu thick and tasted very delicious. Jirokichi was asked if he got drunk on coconut wine. He laughed and said, "No."

There was a fruit tree that they called breadfruit. The tree was about five ken tall and the branches spread out for about an equal distance. The leaves, as well as the fruit, were perfectly round. The fruit was seven or eight sun in diameter just like a child's head. The color was blue-green. The natives would put it in a fire---like chestnuts or bread, and it tasted about the same.

The suho [kao] tree grew to a height of about one io, the diameter of the trunk was about six sun. The branches, as well as the leaves, were green. Sheep liked to eat the round-shaped leaves. The flowers were yellow and shaped like cherry blossoms. The lumber of the kao tree, along with sugar cane, were the island's main products.

The cactus was called maina in the islands. They were numerous and grew to large proportions. The trunk branched out into "leaves" the shape of the palm of one's hand. The trunk was as thick as the size made when one spreads out their arms as if they were full. The cactus was not used for eating but the leaves that hung down were picked, dried and then braided for flowered mats. Foreign people used them for rugs in their homes, and some were shipped abroad. The mats were also called maina.

Hemp palm hair grown in the islands was used to make pure white rope. This rope was strong as well as beautiful. Westerners praised it for its high quality.

Giant bamboo thrived in this warm climate. The spaces between the joints were up to three shaku wide. Natives wove bamboo into baskets and fans.

The staple food in the Sandwich Islands was poi made from taro, a kind of potato. The color of the stem and leaves was the same as the Japanese sato [potato]. They were huge, sometimes two shaku long. A big strong man could not carry more than four at one time on his shoulders.

To prepare poi, natives first dug a hole in the ground, and some pieces of metal were arranged as a kind of oven. A wood fire was prepared in the ground and stones were placed here and there. The taro was put on top of the stones and then the oven arrangement was completely covered with earth. When the taro was thought to be thoroughly baked, they took it out and tasted it. If it was done, it was put into a big mortar that was shaped like a dugout canoe. It was six shaku long, one shaku, six sun wide, and the two people sat who worked the pestle. The pestle was about seven sun long becoming narrower in the middle and made of stone. It was manipulated with both hands.

Beside the mortar was a big gourd about one shaku in diameter filled with water. The two people facing each other worked the pestle vigorously while sometimes pouring water in the taro mixture. When the mixture became sticky like paste it was removed from the mortar and put in the gourds. When eating it the natives simply scooped it up with the index and middle fingers. It was a rather troublesome food for the tropics, however, because it would spoil in a half day's time in hot weather. Jirokichi said he came to like it after a while. It tasted like potato, and if eaten with sugar it was quite tasty. One time when the Japanese were invited to go for an outing in the mountains with some Kanakas, they showed consideration for the visitors by saying, "Since Japanese people are not accustomed to eating poi, we will take watermelon and muskmelon for you."

Rice and Chinese millet [panicum miliaceum] grew abundantly there. They could reap three harvests a year in this mild climate. The rice grains were about three bu long. The Japanese were told that much rice was grown in the Boston area, so they thought that "rice country" was an appropriate name for America.[7] But in America and Russia they didn't eat much rice. In preparing it, they boiled it well until it was like rice gruel and then served it with butter, meat, vegetables, etc. This was eaten with a spoon and called "soup."

Jirokichi was shown two pictures of pineapples. He was told that the plants grew wild on the footpaths of the potato fields. The roots resembled those of the potato plant. They said that the fruit had a good taste. [This was a mistake in understanding.]

Bread was broken up in pieces and put in hot sugar water and it then expanded to three times its previous size. It was very delicious. Tea was imported from China in sealed copper tins. In foreign countries tea is a special commodity and not freely used. The color of the tea was lighter than that in Japan.

Good wine was also quite dear abroad. One bottle would cost something equal to three ryo [gold coins]. Rum wine was considered first class.

American and English people liked a kind of tobacco called merashi [phonetic spelling].[8] It was tobacco that had been preserved in sugar. The Japanese were shown how tobacco was prepared. The leaves were dried for only one day, so they were still somewhat green. Then they were rolled to the thickness of one's finger, or they were twisted like a rope. Sometimes the leaves were stacked up with sugar sprinkled between the layers so it would soak in. Once again they were arranged in layers in a square box and amply sprinkled with sugar water. A cover was put on it and a potter's wheel was used as a press. Then they were rolled or twisted or left in that shape. Also they sometimes piled up the leaves in layers and cut them in the shape of the charcoal sticks used in Japanese calligraphy [like rectangular cigars]. Then they were dried.

Sailors always joked about how much they liked tobacco. Each man carried some in his hip pocket, and when he wanted to use it, he scraped off a little and put it in his mouth and chewed it. They also crushed it in the palm of their hands until it was like dust and put it in their pipes and smoked it.

Somewhere in the Sandwich Islands the Japanese attended an exhibition where they saw a picture of a rhinoceros tied up in a cage. They were told it was a strong and ferocious beast. Also a print made in America and brought from China showed sixteen men seated on the back of such an animal having a drinking party. A band accompanied their singing. The names of the musicians were written on the picture.

They were also shown a picture from America of a horse with no hoofs. It was the same shape as an ordinary horse, but somewhat bigger. They were told that American soldiers rode this type of strong and spirited horse on the battlefield.

A roba [donkey] was called a kamina in the islands. It was smaller than a horse with ears over one shaku long. If a person mounted the animal and it refused to move, the rider moved back to the rump and then it would run.

The drifters were told that there was a kind of fox [?] in America which emitted poison [skunk]. Farmers regarded it as a great nuisance as they sometimes came into their gardens and threw off a terrible stench. It was not only very offensive to the nose, but if it got on one's clothes the odor penetrated the material and it took up to ten days to remove it. When this happened they would run home and bury their clothes in the ground and then soak in a medicinal bath until the stench disappeared.

In the sugar cane fields in the Sandwich Islands there were many lizards. If one wasn't careful when walking through the fields, they might step on them. In the Boston area, the drifters heard, there were lizards as big as serpents and they inflicted harm on people. An American showed the Japanese a picture of the beasts [alligators].

On Oahu island the Japanese saw a salt producing plant. On a narrow strip of land jutting out into the sea, the rocks had been scraped down until there was a flat indentation about 200 ken long, 100 ken wide and one shaku deep. A waterway led from it to the sea at the end of which there was a gate to regulate the flow of water during ebb and flood tides. During a flood tide the water was let in until it was about five sun deep. Then the gate was firmly closed. For about ten days it was left like that and during that time the sun evaporated the moisture and hard white salt remained. Salt could be produced in this way twice a month. The hardened salt was about two sun five bu thick. This was dug out and smashed into small pieces and put in straw bags. The bags were of various sizes holding one or two to and one to five sho each.

For table salt the lumps were put in a mortar and ground until it was like pure white snow. The method of evaporation for producing salt could be used both here and in Tahiti, they said, but not in a temperate zone. Only places between 23° N. and 23° S. latitude were warm enough for making salt in this manner.

Unlike the Japanese, Westerners were fond of eating meat. One foreigner said to Jirokichi, "If it is a hoofless animal, all of its meat can be eaten. When you return to Japan you should tell your countrymen that."

There were many stock farms on Oahu, some very expansive and others not so big. In the outskirts of Honolulu at the south end of the harbor there was a slaughterhouse for cows. Southeast of it was a big storehouse for hides. One day the Japanese were invited to see the process of capturing and slaughtering cattle. Ranchers kept their cattle in pens surrounded by wooden fences or stone walls. These pens were from 70 to 80 ken to 100 ken square. In the daytime the gate was left open so the cows were free to graze in the pasture, but in the evening they were driven back into the enclosure. The owners made a small slash in the cows' ears, or they burned brands on their rear ends, for identification purposes.

Wild cattle in the Sandwich Islands were especially ferocious and difficult to capture. Two men on horseback would lasso them with a rope that was as thick as a man's thumb and about ten fathoms long.[9] If the rope was thrown skillfully, the loop on the end would coil around the horns of the beast. The cow's legs would spread out on the ground and it could not get away. The cowboy whipped the horse to make it run faster as the cow was dragged away. The other man struck the cow repeatedly as they drove it toward the slaughterhouse.

The slaughterhouse was built right at the water's edge. It was a wooden hut about two ken square with a peaked roof. The foundation posts had been covered with copper sheeting before they were driven in the sand. Boards about five sun wide and three sun thick covered the floor. They were laid so there were gaps from two to three bu between them. About nine shaku from the door attached to the floor boards, was a post with a big iron ring that was two sun in diameter and about as thick as one's thumb. There was another post outside about three ken from the hut to which an iron ring was attached about four <u>shaku</u> from the ground. The cow was first tied up there.

The cow looked at its captors with great wrath and tried to attack. After it had settled down and become calmer a man tied a rope around its back legs and took the other end of the rope into the hut and put it through the ring of the post inside. Some five man took hold of the rope and while putting all their strength together they pulled the cow inside the hut. The animal skidded and tumbled this way and that and finally fell over. The slaughterer immediately stabbed it in the neck with a dagger, the cow let out one cry, and it went limp. Blood gushed out like a fountain. The slaughterer trampled on the body while turning round and round in order to get all the blood out. The blood flowed between the floor boards and into the sea.

Only two men were required for the butchering process. When the blood was all out of the carcass, a brass pestle-shaped mallet and a knife around five <u>bu</u> wide and five <u>sun</u> long was used to strip off the hide. In places where there was hard gristle they used a hammer to get it out, and then they discarded it.

When all the skin was removed a crossbar was inserted between the hind legs, and a rope was fastened to it. The rope was put through a pulley and the carcass was hung head-down from the ceiling. The underside was split open then and the internal organs were scooped out and fell into a wooden tub. (This was the butcher's share). After that, the two men gripped the handles of a saw to cut off the horns and hoofs. Then they sawed through the bones and meat to divide the carcass into pieces for commercial use. Sometimes they had to use a hatchet to cut through the joints. One cow was usually cut up into twelve pieces. The pieces were put in a bucket for delivery to the owner. If the meat was sold to dealers, it was first weighed at the slaughterhouse. Chinese firms, which sometimes had as many as 100 employees, needed one head of cattle for food each day.

About 30 <u>ken</u> from the slaughterhouse was Mr. Barney's [phonetic spelling] cowhide storehouse.[10] The building was

six or seven <u>ken</u> deep and five <u>ken</u> wide. It was about five
<u>ken</u> high. It was located at the seaside so the hides could be
exposed to the hot sun. It was said that Mr. Barney made a
great profit from selling hides.

One day Mr. Barney invited the Japanese party to his
home. In spite of his being a very wealthy man, he was
friendly and hospitable to the sailors. He welcomed them
with a handshake and offered a light meal. Just at that time
construction was almost completed on a big new office
building for his company. Jirokichi thought that such a
building would be inconceivable in Japan. Many tenement
homes were in his compound to house the servants he had
bought up among the islanders. They were kept busy every
day carrying money from one establishment to another for
this millionaire.

Mr. Barney told Jirokichi's party about having helped
the drifters from Echigo who came to the islands in 1832 get
back to Japan via Sitka. Jirokichi pleaded with him to help
them, too. He promised he would do all he could to find a
means for them to get home. Then he added, "If you return
safely, please give my regards to them [the Echigo party].

Beside some company buildings windmills were erected.
They were constructed in various ways. One type was
described by Jirokichi:

First a tall wooden enclosure was built over the well.
One side was flush with the kitchen wall so that when the
outlet was open they could have running water inside.

The wooden enclosure was erected in the shape of a
trapezoid, wider at the base than the top. When constructing
it, four big posts were first set up on the ground. Then
horizontal crossbars were nailed on. Between the upper and
lower crossbars vertical crossbars were attached in the shape
of the letter <u>ju</u> [the character for "ten" or the shape of the
plus sign +] for reinforcement. Boards were then nailed to the
frame. At the top, as well as a little way down from the top,
wooden supports in the shape of the letter <u>ii</u> [the character for

"wall" or the shape of #]. These were braces that held fast the platform for the fans.

A lattice grating covered the well. Through the center of this a long wooden conduit was inserted. The conduits varied in height and shape; some were hexagon-shaped and others were octagonal. One end reached the water in the well and the other extended over the top of the trapezoid. Water gushed out through this conduit but it could be regulated.

To that conduit the windmill blades were attached. Two wooden slats were put together which could be opened or closed according to the velocity of the wind. When the wind was strong only one side was needed. The number of blades varied on different windmills. The windmill Jirokichi described had two fans revolving on iron axes on either side. Extending below and holding up the axes were two iron rods. The # shaped framework at the top of the trapezoid held the rods in place so they did not move.

Near where the axis was joined with the fan it bent at a right angle. From the point where it turned a long iron rod came down through the center of the water conduit into the well. At the end of this rod there was a wooden block attached to it with a hook. In the middle of the block there was a valve that opened and closed. When the fans rotated the vertical part of the axis went up and down causing the valve to open and close and thus regulating the flow of water.

Rev. Bingham was a man of high morals according to Jirokichi. He was also extremely clever, but humble. He did everything from needlework to chopping wood. He seemed to be busy all day long, his body never stopped moving. His leisure time was spent doing things he enjoyed most. When he lived on the outer islands he raised horses and hired the natives to exercise them.

He explained to Jirokichi how he went about educating the islanders. He used only 14 letters of the English alphabet. The Hawaiian language has five vowels and seven consonants. He said that the Christian missionaries had just recently

[1839] succeeded in translating the Bible into the language of the islands.

The missionaries had their own printing plant next to Dr. Judd's home. Foreign books were all done by the type-printing method. The type was one <u>bu</u> square and five <u>bu</u> long. A letter was carved on the end of the slender bar. First the typesetter gathered up the type bars and set them in place in special frame. A proofreader checked for errors and revised it. When the proofreading was done the printing was carried out by two people. But all together the task of making a book required ten people, including the binders. The book cover was usually made of sheepskin.

The printing press was a big piece of equipment, but it could be easily dismantled and transported from place to place. The apparatus was six or seven <u>shaku</u> high with two separate vertical iron rods one <u>sun</u>, five <u>bu</u> square about six <u>shaku</u> apart. A horizontal bar was attached to them near the top. The vertical rods were set in heavy bases on which some letters were carved. These bases were bell-shaped, the lower part being about three <u>shaku</u> in diameter. The ends of both the horizontal and vertical rods were curved like a bent hand. In the center of the horizontal bar there was a ring through which the center vertical rod, which was attached to the printing plate moved up and down. Near the top of the center vertical rod another rod, bent in the shape of a bow, was attached with screws. This bow-shaped rod extended down to the base of the vertical rod on the left. It was seven or eight <u>shaku</u> long and about five <u>bu</u> thick.

Near the base of the vertical rod [on the right] there was a curved crosspiece which was a support for a stand that held a porcelain pot filled with ink.

The printing plate was about five <u>bu</u> thick. From the lower, part of the center rod three support rods spread out and were attached to the cover of the plate. A little above them there was a bent grip. The bottom surface of the printing plate was covered with woolen cloth.

For printing they used a paint brush or a roller with an iron handle to apply the ink. The roller was five <u>sun</u> in diameter and one <u>shaku</u> seven or eight <u>sun</u> long. The outside was wrapped in thick cloth. When they pushed it, it went round and round over the plate.

Under the press board the type had been set in a leather frame placed on an iron stand. The leather frame had a cover attached which was lined with woolen cloth on the undersurface. The frame was folded double from top to bottom. Both had a cover attached so they could be opened or closed. Paper was piled up beside the printing press.

Well, as for the printing process the leather frame was set on the iron stand in the center. The type was set firmly in orderly rows. The roller which had been dipped in ink would have to rotate just once over the surface. They said that three or four sheets of paper could be printed with just one application of ink. [Koga found this hard to believe.] After the ink was smeared on the plate the top frame was let down to keep the type in place. The face of the type was higher than the frame. [This was to protect the part of the paper resting on the frame from getting soiled by the ink.] Then the paper was set on top of the type and the cover was let down. With the handle near the spread out rods the cover was pressed down and beautiful printing could be done.

To print big plates such as maps they used a lithograph process. The picture was engraved on a big stone about six <u>shaku</u> long and three <u>shaku</u> wide. The upper surface of the fine-textured stone was smooth and pure white. This was set on a four-legged wooden stand with a wooden cover. For moving the heavy plate they had to use a pulley. In the case of using copper plates the same process was used.

The print shop was in a big building. They worked only in the daytime so the building was locked at night. No one was allowed to live there because of the heat from the fire.

The Japanese thought that culture was now flourishing in the Sandwich Islands. They observed that many written materials were being published in Lahaina. Jirokichi said that western people criticized the Japanese and Chinese woodblock process as being awkward and crude saying, "By our country's method letters are carved piece by piece so the same type can be used over and over again." (Jirokichi did not know much about Japan's printing process, so he could not answer. Of course they thought their tintype method was superior to the woodblock process.)

Westerners used quill pens with brass nibs for calligraphy. When they write with ink, at first there is no impression, but in a few moments it becomes black. For ordinary writing they use pencils made by putting graphite inside of long slender pieces of wood. The end is sharpened for writing. The impression is lighter than charcoal. Pencils only cost about 1/16 a ryo for a dozen. Children sometimes used roofing slates to practice handwriting instead of paper. They used a slate pencil and when they wanted to erase it they simply spit on the slate and wiped it off with a rag.

When the drifters were in the Sandwich Islands they witnessed a surgical operation in which the patient's eyeball was removed. First the patient was tied down tightly with leather straps at the head and around the abdomen. Only the afflicted eye was exposed. The doctors had over 400 kinds of surgical instruments. Among them was a special small knife that was used to scoop out the eyeball. After removing it the eye socket was packed with an ointment. In about 50 days the patient had completely recovered. The Japanese were told that if the patient had not had the operation, he would have lost the sight of the other eye, too.

The house in which the drifters lived was made of adobe. The adobe was very simply made. First a pool of clay mud was made about one ken in diameter. To this mud they added grass that had been chopped up in small pieces. That mixture was then put in wooden frames. Since it was usually hot the clay dried quickly. By the time they had finished filling up about ten frames, the first frame was completely hardened. In this way they continued to empty and refill the frames.

The adobe bricks were piled up until they were about six <u>shaku</u> high and then mud was patted on with the palm of the hand to make them stick together. The bricks were set on a slant at the top of the walls and were scraped and sharpened to look like a roof. The roofs of adobe houses were not made of tile, usually they were simply covered with grass. The Kanakas and Chinese often used this type of construction.

Jirokichi's party stayed at the Cantonese merchant's home until December [1839] in Honolulu. One day he told them that they should go to Maui Island where his brother John had set up a sugar manufacturing business in Wailuku. He added, "I am sure that there will be no warships coming into this port at least until January, so I think it would be best for you to go and work at my brother's place for a while.[11]

After the Japanese were reassured that word would be sent to them immediately upon the arrival of any ships going to China, four of them, including Jirokichi, Hachizaemon, Rokubei and Shichizaemon, set out for Maui.

Chapter V

TO MAUI AND RETURN TO OAHU

Curiosities and treasures
So many wondrous things
Now half are forgotten.

Upon arriving in Lahaina the Japanese were told that the sugar cane on the plantation in Wailuku was not yet ripe enough for harvesting, so they were told to stay in Lahaina for a while. At this place they were again accommodated by the good offices of Rev. Baldwin.

It was at this remote corner of the world where the drifters saw in the New Year. The Ken, the island's chief magistrate, invited the Japanese to his residence for the holiday festivities which started off with cannon fire. Crowds of Islanders gathered for eating, drinking and merrymaking throughout the day.

The drifters sometimes attended church services while they were staying with Rev. Baldwin. About a half ri from the church, at the foot of a mountain, there was a school. Since the teacher of that school sometimes came to church, the Japanese were familiar with him. One day Jirokichi, Shichizaemon and Hachizaemon went to visit the school where they were shown many rare things.[1]

The teacher was glad to see them and was very hospitable to the Japanese. At the time of their visit the twenty pupils were engaged in a scientific experiment that taught them the principle of combustion. They were spinning a small generator by hand. By using a device in which something like a citron seed was set in the hold of something that looked like a branch of coral [details are obscure] they were shown how combustion takes place.

Also the Japanese were shown something curious in a glass bottle. There were five or six long white objects that looked like candles soaking in water. For an experiment, they were taken out and put on a piece of paper. Instantly steam arose from them. The teacher said, "If we were to leave them here a little bit longer, they would have burned up." Also, when he scraped off pieces of the material and pounded them on an anvil, light was diffused and sparks flew as far as Jirokichi's head. Somewhat alarmed, Jirokichi asked, "What is that used for?" The teacher answered, "In times of emergency, they can be thrown at the enemy, or in wartime they can be used to set fire to the enemy's encampments." He added that thousands of the explosive devices were stored in a rocky cave. They were kept in water that had to be changed twice a day because if the water boiled down they would be likely to explode. Then the teacher added, "Isn't this stored in the Japanese capital as well?" Jirokichi answered that he supposed it was but he was only a sailor and didn't know much about such things.[2]

When they were staying at Dr. Judd's house in Honolulu they noticed that he had two or three of the explosive devices in his possession, too.

The three drifters were also shown a triangular-shaped glass object [prism?] which emitted various colored rays of light. Then the teacher took them to a room where there were specimens of various kinds of shellfish and stones. The Japanese compared them with Japanese varieties and eagerly asked questions and took notes. In this school students were taught astronomy, surveying, etc. They also studied anatomy. The Japanese saw a full-length human skeleton as well as a mummy.

When Rokubei went sightseeing one day with two or three native residents at the church he was shown many rare things. There was something like a jewel set up on top of a stand, whatever it was spun round and round. The visitors all joined hands, then the person on the end held out a short pole and touched the jewel-like object. As soon as the object was touched everyone felt a tingling sensation go through their bodies at the same time which made them automatically drop their hands immediately.

They saw many other rare things which interested them but they could no longer remember them.

Well, one day the Japanese were paddled to Lahaina on the other side of the mountain by seven Kanakas in a canoe. They maneuvered the boat so skillfully it utterly flew over the water. In Wailuku they were taken to John's shop. One or two months after their arrival his storehouse burned down. This building was six or seven <u>ken</u> deep and about five <u>ken</u> wide. Sugar and grain were stored in it at the time of the fire. He also lost a beautiful big dining room table that craftsmen had spent many days making with great care. The intensity of the fire was so great that one could only see as far as one's hand. Fire fighters could no nothing but wring their hands as the blaze burned beyond control. It was said that John suffered a loss of over 2000 <u>ryo</u>.

The heat was unbearable in Wailuku. The Japanese said that when they took a bath the towel would dry instantly. There wasn't any cold drinking water to quench their thirst so they had to chew on sugar cane. It tasted cool and sweet.

On the whole sugar cane grew naturally on this island but the Chinese were the first to cut and press it. Here the Japanese were to spend about three months helping erect a small building to house the sugar pressing equipment. From talking to the natives, the Japanese came to realize that this was a remote place. They knew that there was no way of finding out if and when a warship came to Honolulu. They went to the local pastor to whom they expressed their fervent desire to return to Oahu. He said, "If a warship comes, surely you will be notified, so stay here for a while."

In the meantime the small building in which the sugar pressing equipment had been placed also caught fire. The Japanese helped in trying to extinguish it but because of a strong wind it burned down and John suffered another big loss. Among the equipment he lost was a waterwheel which had been shipped from England.

As for the sugar producing process, first the ground was dug up and cultivated for the sugar cane. A small factory was built to manufacture sugar. This 20 ken by ten ken building was three cho from the city. It was divided into two parts. Two stone mills were on one side and two big cauldrons were on the other.

The stalks were first put into the mill which was usually operated by two oxen. In Oahu a horse was used and sometimes human beings. In the latter case, three to eighteen people were needed to turn the pestle. Among them were many women. The women had been assigned this job as punishment for having commited lewd acts. Sometimes they had to continue this kind of work for as long as ten months. They were really treated like beasts.

In the mortar there was a wooden device connected to a rope attached to the animal. A man drove the horse or ox with a whip. If it did not move, he beat it with the whip. Another man stood between the two mills thrusting the stalks in. As the device went round, the stalks were crushed and juice flowed outside the mortar into a trough. Another worker gathered up the stalks that dropped outside the mortar and took them to the man thrusting them into the crusher. This time they were inserted in the opposite direction. By crushing them from both ends the juice was completely squeezed out.

The juice flowed from the stone trough to a big kettle lying on its side, and finally flowed into a barrel. With a big dipper it was then ladled out into an iron cauldron and brought to a boil. Many bubbles formed on the surface of the juice, so they put something that looked like our aburakasu [literally "oil cake"---soybean dregs after the oil has been squeezed out] and the juice was beaten with a spatula until the bubbles disappeared.

After the juice was boiled down, water was put into a clay pot nearby and with the spatula the stock was taken out and tested in this water. They pinched it between two fingers to see if it had hardened to the right consistency.

An eight to pot shaped like a funnel that tapered down to a tube only about one sun two or three bu was prepared to receive the juice. The neck was stopped up with a bundle of cane stalks. When the juice was poured into the funnel pot, it was strained through the stalks and then it dripped into a wooden tub below. A cover was put on the tub and it was left that way overnight.

The next morning the stalks were removed from the neck of the post. The juice in the tub had become white sugar. If the sugar was not white enough, they put wheat or barley straw that had been soaked in water in the funnel and the stock was poured over it.

The sugar was left in the tub for seven or eight days. Then the hardened mass was turned out on a wooden block and smashed with a wooden mallet. Later it was put through a sieve and then let dry for another day before it was packaged for shipment. The nectar was poured into a barrel and both were shipped abroad. When the demand was high the manufacturing process continued day and night.

For making rock sugar, some white powder was added during the manufacturing process. The boiled down mixture and the sugar juice were poured into a shallow iron mold that was about three shaku square and one sun deep. The mold had been partitioned off with strips of metal beforehand and strings were stretched across going through each parition. When the sugar had hardened like a stone the metal partitions were removed and the one sun-square sugar cubes were taken out. The corners were rounded off and the strings connecting them were tied together like a string of beads. They were also put in wooden boxes and shipped abroad.

Tasaburo had the job of thrusting the sugar cane stalks into the mill. Kinzo first drove the oxen but later helped a Chinese named Kameyama [phonetic spelling] boil down the sugar. [This is strange because Kinzo and Tasaburo were not among the party that went to John's place. This may have been another time and place.]

The Japanese also saw a new apparatus for crushing sugar cane. This machine had been shipped from England. It was so big and heavy that it had to be delivered on a wagon drawn by seven or eight head of oxen. The mechanism was made up of three three-shaku long and two-shaku wide vertical iron rollers. The rollers would rotate against each other and squeeze the cane. When the crosspiece on the middle roller was rotated by an ox or a horse, the other two rollers would go round. Thus the cane could be crushed in two places at once.

In May [1840] the drifters received word from Oahu that a warship had come into port. They fairly jumped for joy at the news and said to John, "We wish to leave right away." He looked rather skeptical and replied, "I think that message is a mistake. Since you are making enough money here, why don't you stay?"[3]

But Jirokichi, along with Rokubei, Shichizaemon and Hachizaemon forcibly got some time off and managed to flee from John's place. They made their way on foot over the mountain to Lahaina. the eight-ri trek was nearly inaccessible and there was no water. Because of the intense heat they got so thirsty they had to resort to smashing mosquito larvae in order to moisten their lips. After suffering unbearable hardships they finally made it to Lahaina. [According to Tokei Monogatari, Jirokichi's party spent about 20 days here and at that time visited Lanai and observed the salt producing facilities there. This is not mentioned in Bandan.]

From Lahaina port the Japanese were taken to Honolulu by canoe. On the way they said they could see two islands--Lanai and Taorabe.[4] When they arrived at Honolulu they could see a French ship anchored off shore. It was not so big but the three masts were big and sturdy. Gun emplacements were set up on both sides of the ship. There were also two American warships there which were equipped with 2nd and 3rd class gun emplacements. Upon seeing the heavily-armed ships the Japanese thought: go now, there is the danger of war. They were told that the French ship was originally scheduled to go to Canton, but upon hearing that the Opium War had recently broken out in China, they changed their minds. Now it was going to America.

The Islanders paddled out in canoes to see the ships anchored in the offing. Passengers were asked to pay 60 cents for the ride, but the Japanese were not expected to pay because they were visitors. Jirokichi's party enthusiastically joined the observers on the French warship. Upon seeing the caps and uniforms of the French sailors the Japanese at first thought they looked Chinese. They could walk freely all around the ship where big cannons and other munitions were placed.[5]

There was another warship in the harbor that had sailed past New Zealand and near the frozen sea of the Antarctica.   The hull had been damaged and was being repaired at the shipyards in Honolulu.

One day Jirokichi watched the preparations for making repairs on a big ship. There was an inclined platform at the beach made of big timbers laid parallel to the water like a big shelf.   This structure was 14 or 15 <u>ken</u> long and five <u>ken</u> wide. Copper-covered piles partly under water supported the platform.

When preparing the ship for repairs first they removed the upper parts of the masts. Then heavy ropes were wound around the bases of all three masts.   The ends of the ropes were connected to a big pulley on shore.   Support rods were then attached to both sides of the underside of the hull to keep the ship upright.   Also two big squared timbers that had been hollowed out in the exact shape of the ship were attached lengthwise on either side of the bottom of the hull.

Many head of oxen or horses were borrowed from local farmers to pull the ropes, and the ship was moved up on the dry dock. A raised platform was used to repair damage to the sheet copper covering the bottom.

When the repairs were finished once more the ship was lowered into the sea. Beforehand an inclined plane was made with heavy timbers. This was long or short depending on the

size of the ship. A short one was over 20 <u>ken</u>. On top of the
slip there were two U-shaped gutter rails placed there to
prevent the ship from moving from side to side. The support
rods attached to the underside of the hull were removed and
then two long squared timbers exactly fitting the ship's
bottom were attached in lengthwise positions. These were
usually about 2/3 the length of the ship's hull. If the ship
was 20 <u>ken</u> long, the timbers were 14 or 15 <u>ken</u>, they said.
Those used for a two-mast ship were about one <u>shaku</u> five <u>sun</u>
square. For a one-mast ship they used one-<u>shaku</u> square
timbers. On both sides of the timbers there were iron rings.
They were used when moving the ship along the slip.

Before the ship launching the support rods on either
side of the hull were removed. The copper sheeting was
lightly nailed to the bottom, then after the launching it was
securely attached again.

Well, the ship had been tied up with heavy tow ropes.
many people lined up on each side of the ship taking hold of
the ropes. Putting their strength together they all pulled at
once to move the ship. From a high place on the ship, the
ship's head carpenter held a megaphone and shouted when to
pull the rope in order to make sure they pulled in unison.
Then when they let go, the ship slid down the slip and floated
into the sea. As the rails on the slip and the ship's bottom
were made to fit exactly the ship could slide down the
platform just like a sliding door slides along a threshold. To
make it slide more easliy they poured cows' or pigs' grease in
the grooves beforehand. The spikes securing the copper
sheeting on the bottom of the ship had been loosely affixed
before launching so now the cover was securely attached
again.

In the case of a newly constructed ship, a priest was
called to the scene to offer prayers for calm seas before the
launching. Also, a merry reception was held at which the
guests could drink to their heart's content. Even passing
acquaintances were treated to alcoholic beverages on the
festive occasion.

When merchant ships were heavily loaded the draft was deep. The apertures of the cannons on the lower deck were kept closed when not in use because they were almost level with the surface of the water. Warships were not so heavily loaded, so their draft was not so deep. Most of the ship came up over the surface of the water and the eyes of the cannons were kept open. Cannons were set up on the 2nd and 3rd decks. A big warship had as many as 160 cannons. The French had warships on which cannons were placed only on the 1st deck.

The body of the man-of-war was very big and tall and it was equipped with many cannons. When the cannons were not in use the gun barrels were placed in a vertical position toward the sky. The aperture was one shaku four or five sun and the overall length was one jo. There were also small cannons with apertures less than six sun in diameter. The projectiles were called "chain shots"---two balls were connected with an iron chain. Each ball weighed 12 kamme. The chain was about as thick as a man's index finger, the length ranged from three to five ken to ten ken. The Japanese were told that when one of these chain shots was fired, an entire company of soldiers, or a house, could be destroyed instantly. Because of this foreign people were very cautious about using them.

Jirokichi's party witnessed a cannon firing drill one time. Three people were required to fire a cannon on a warship. One person took charge of the gunpowder, another man's duty was to clean the gun barrel, and the other did the aiming. They put cotton in their ears as a protection from the intense noise, and they all wound cotton cloths firmly around their bellies when they were on lighting duty. The kickback when firing came back as much as two shaku, pulling on the strong rope with which the cannon was secured to the gunwale of the ship. If too much gunpowder was put in the cannon, it could overturn, so the man on lighting duty was careful not to stand directly behind the cannon. For the firing that Jirokichi witnessed 24 or 25 small projectiles were bound by copper wire in a bundle. When the cannon was fired the projectiles fell over a wide area.

When the cannon was not being used the barrel was packed with burlap cloth, but even then it was dangerous to go near it. One time three Sandwich Islanders carelessly walked into the cannon's line of fire when it was stuffed with cloth and the cannon accidently went off. Pieces of cloth flew all over the place and the natives suffered burns on the head and face.

Gunpowder was stored in a hole in the ground. A rounded mound of earth covered it, making it look like a natural hill. On one side of the mound there was a an entranceway that was always kept locked. Armed soldiers guarded it night and day. There was a hut near the powder magazine where guards could rest.

In the Sandwich Islands trading ships from every country were always coming and going. World news could be transmitted in this way as quickly as ten days.

One time when the drifters were talking with Rev. Bingham in his home they heard that there had been a big fire in Osaka. It was unbelievable to the sailors that it was possible to hear news of their homeland when they were thousands of ri away. He told them that the fire had been started by someone named Oshio.[6] At first, relief supplies were brought on whaling ships to Nagasaki, so the news was probably brought by them. Warships also conveyed international news.

When Jirokichi's party was in Honolulu an American said to them, "The poor Japanese people cannot go to foreign countries, so they are the same as a frog in a well." He added, Japan is tomachan [This may be phonetic spelling for 'too much'] so your countrymen are prohibited from going abroad. Also you only have rice for food and if there is a year with a poor harvest, the people will starve. You people, too, when you return home should not eat only rice," he warned them. In the West, wheat was the main crop and rice was second, according to Jirokichi.

Another person criticized Japan for its attitude toward drifters saying, "If we take drifters back to their country, cannons are fired at us. It's an utterly ridiculous country. It is the same as if I took a lost child back to its home and the parents threw stones at me. In a sense you are children of the Ken ['King'---he should have said 'Emperor'], right? If a person takes you home, he should receive a handshake.[7]

One time an English soldier bragged to Jirokichi about the power of the British. "Now there are 270 or 280 English warships attacking China's Canton. [He was referring to the Opium War.] When this war ends we will approach the Ryukyu Island [Okinawa] and Japan." Jirokichi shook with fear upon hearing his words and immediately went to an American warship captain and asked him about this. "Oh, he is just a soldier running off at the mouth," he said. "You shouldn't believe everything he says. That may not be true, but if there is a war in the seas around Japan and a Japanese ship meets with a warship, the food as well as the rest of the cargo may be confiscated for military use. One cannot escape such an action because it is a wartime regulation."

An American also told Jirokichi, "Long ago [actually about sixty years before] the English were defeated in a war [Revolutionary War] but now they attack with ruthless destruction. Because of their great military power, English people always assume an overbearing attitude toward others. That brutal characteristic I do not like at all." The Japanese heard such criticism from the Russians, too. They thought that maybe there might be some envy of the great power of the English in their words. Jirokichi did not understand exactly but he thought that some points of what they said were probably true.

The Japanese were told that as many as 4000 or 5000 ships came and went in London harbor every day. They heard that England is already in possession of three-quarters of the world. In another hundred years they think the entire world will be unified under the English. Jirokichi realized, however, that at this time the United States was getting strong too and people must be aware of the situation.

Jirokichi also heard that in recent years the English occupied an island 300 ri from Ise Bay in Japan. 400 or 500 people are stationed there to guard it. This was thought to have been an uninhabited island. [Ogasawara or Bonin Islands.] Now many Americans live there. Jirokichi said to the foreigner who told him about it, "Why did they do that?' He smiled and answered, "In this way we will close in on Japan." [Koga added his doubt to this statement.][8]

One day Dr. Judd talked to the Japanese about Chrisitanity in their country. While looking at a book he said, "About 340 or 350 years ago <u>bateran</u> [padres--Catholic missionary priests] went to Japan. Do you know about that? The drifters replied, "We heard stories about it from our elders." They smiled and added, "Those <u>bateran</u> were people from a place called Luzon, south of the Ryukyu Islands [the Phillipines]. They used the name 'Christians' just to get into Japan. They appropriated much money for themselves. At this time Japan had an excellent 'king' and he ordered them to leave. Chrisitanity is a religion that teaches compassion and good conduct."[9]

Dr. Judd showed the drifters a world map with the names "India" and many other countries written on it. Japanese place names were in <u>katakana</u>. He also had a detailed map of Japan showing the degrees of latitude and lonitude. A six-<u>sun</u> square represented one degree on this map. The exact route to enter and leave Uraga harbor and the depth of the water was clearly shown. Also the harbor entrance down to the number of rocks the foreigners knew well. Dr. Judd said, "This channel is only a few miles wide and there are mountains on both sides. On top of these mountains the Japanese have cannon emplacements so we need to be careful when we approach the harbor by ship."

Jirokichi said, "Not only Uraga, but on every seacoast of Japan there are cannons set up to guard against foreign intruders. It would make an invasion very difficult."

Dr. Judd shook his head and replied, "No, no, that's nonsense. We know all about it in detail."

Also on that day Dr. Judd read from a text about Japanese places. Among those that he mentioned were Kaga

[Ishikawa prefecture], Noto, Ecchu [Toyama], etc. There was also a map on which only the shorelines of various provinces were drawn. In the Ecchu area two lines were drawn to show a river.

According to Jirokichi's words, foreigners think that Japan regards all other countries as enemies. Whenever they see a foreign ship, regardless of its purpose, they fire upon it immediately. Therefore many countries look upon Japan as a "mad dog." Whenever they approach Japanese territory they do it with deep vigilance, and they carefully arrange arms. The more the foreign countries build up their military preparedness, the more the Japanese regard them as aggressors, and the people on both sides regard each other with hostility as a result.

Jirokichi met foreigners in the Sandwich Islands who had come near Japan when the ship they were on was anchored at a port near the Tsugaru Straits. According to their explanation, for no reason at all, as soon as the Japanese saw the ship they began shooting at them. The angry foreigners let down a boat and rowed to shore. When they quickly raided a cannon positioned on a hill, the guards were so taken aback that they fled from the scene. Upon examining the cannon, the foreigners found out it was made of wood. It was only coated with a lacquer varnish to make it look like copper. They were amused to discover that the cannons were only spurious weapons. The foreigners then defiantly took the cannon, together with its cart, and pushed it off a cliff while raising their voices in laughter. The narrator of this episode looked at Jirokichi and said, "From this experience, you can see that Japanese cannons are fakes." Jirokichi had no words to reply.[10]

In Honolulu an American warship captain said to Jirokichi one day, "We are thinking of going to Edo one of these days to negotiate for trade." Jirokichi replied, "As for Japan it is already permissible for foreign countries to carry on trade through Nagasaki. You too should go there. It is useless to go to Edo." The captain smiled and said, "No, the 'king' [Shogun], who has the whole country under his countrol is in Edo, so we will go there and ask."

Another American said, "For some time we have been thinking of going to Edo to negotiate for trade. No matter what we have done, consent has been denied. Next time we will demand that our request be granted. Eijiro, [Jirokichi's nickname] if you return home, we will ask you to be our interpreter when our ship lands at the Japanese port." Then he spread out a map of Japan. "Kaga [Jirokichi's home district] and Edo are only this many _ri_ apart. If you hurry you could get there in seven or eight days by horse," he added.[11]

Also the American said, "When we come we would like to get much lacquerware." The drifters noted that Westerners valued Japanese lacquerware very highly. When Jirokichi's party was rescued after the shipwreck the sailors on the James Loper scrambled about to get some lacquerware cups.

The Japanese were also told about Americans who had explored the area around Sakhalin Island. They said that between the Amur River and Sakhalin the ocean was shallow and muddy. Once an American ship went through the Tsugaru Straits and then northward, following the coast of Sakhalin. There were many reefs and shoals, so because of the danger of running aground they turned southwest toward Korea and made observations of that territory.

Just before he returned to America, Rev. Bingham invited Jirokichi to his home one day. He indicated that his guest should sit on a chair facing the sun. Then he placed a large mirror at his side and traced Jirokichi's profile on the surface of the mirror. After that he put a piece of paper on the mirror and rubbed it with his hand. The image was thus transferred to the reverse side of the paper. As he put it in his notebook the pastor said, "Eijiro, I will take your picture to America with me."

When Rev. Bingham left the islands one day in August a great crowd of Kanakas from all over the islands came to the harbor to see him off. As was the custom among western people, cannons were fired. The wailing of the people could still be heard over the cannons' roar. Until the ship was completely out of sight the crowd waved both hands in farewell and cried out, "Maoi! Maoi! Aloha! Aloha!" This was a prayer for peace and good health.[12]

Eleven months had passed since Tasaburo's party had first arrived in Oahu and still no American warship arrived that was bound for China. The two that were in the harbor were going to America.) If they could get on one going to Canton, the Japanese hoped to be able to return to Nagasaki from there. Every day they waited from morning to night and finally they could wait no longer. In July [1840] they earnestly begged Rev. Bingham and Dr. Judd to help them find some means to get home. They said, "We have no way of knowing when a warship will come. Maybe you can get home sooner if you first go to Russian territory rather than wait here. We will arrange for you to get on an English cargo ship going to Kamchatka."

In just a few days the Japanese boarded the <u>Harlequin</u> in Honolulu harbor. It was a nice day so many people came to see them off shouting, "Aloha!" Two cannons were fired on the ship as it headed out of the harbor and headed for Kamchatka peninsula.[13]

Chapter VI

KAMCHATKA

A full beard in the blizzard
Like sparkling threads.

The Harlequin sailed on August 3, 1840 with Captain J. O. Carter and Captain Sen at the helm. Captain Carter had a store in the islands and his cargo consisted of such commodities as sugar, flour, etc. Captain Sen's wife and child were on board as well as other women and children.

The Japanese described Captain Sen as a rough, bearded, unaffected man who was a heavy drinker. According to Jirokichi he was only 24 or 25 years old. If sailors flinched from the cold in the north seas, he showed no sympathy for them, instead he would douse them with icy water.

The drifters were given comfortable accommodations on the ship. Sleeping berths were similar to those on the American ship.[1] The bed frame was pulled out from the wall like a chest of drawers. Each compartment was about two shaku high, four shaku wide and seven shaku long. The beds were just wide enough for the sailors' bodies to fit. The compartments were arranged on the 2nd and 3rd decks. Each bed was covered with a heavy quilt embroidered on both sides, along with three pillows piled up at the head and foot. Westerners had the custom of using pillows for both the head and the feet. A curtain could be drawn across the front making it private. There were glass windows in the ceiling so even at night it was never completely dark.

Above the berth there was a cupboard with two doors that could be opened to the left and to the right. This was for storing foodstuffs and personal belongings. Under the bed there was a storage space for clothing.

For those who could not get used to the ship's pitching and rolling, they had hammocks to sleep in. A piece of canvas about seven or eight <u>shaku</u> long with cords attached on either end was suspended between two poles. The hammocks hung freely in the air so the sailors sleeping in them did not feel the tilting and shaking that one did in an ordinary bed. A lamp was set up beside them and there was a container of live coals for smoking.

The ship's galley or kitchen was constructed in such a way that it was portable. It was about seven <u>shaku</u> square and had a wooden roof. The inside walls were covered with sheet copper. Under the iron stove was a grate on which firewood was arranged.

The stove had an iron door which opened and shut just like a gate. After the fire had begun to burn briskly the door was shut so as to hold in the heat.

On top of the stove there were two big square iron pots which were divided with partitions which fit so snugly that various kinds of cooking could be prepared at the same time with no danger of the gravy stock of one mixing with the taste of the other mixture.

On the left side of the stove there was a drawer. When the cook pulled it out he put fat in it and broiled meat, or baked bread. The heat transmitted to this section was not so intense, so they could be cooked slowly. A hooked device was used to pull out the drawer when it was hot.

Attached to the back of the stove was a copper-covered chimney. It had one bend in it before it reached the ceiling. In case of strong winds they could block the chimney opening with a round tile-like device that looked like the decorative tiles used at the end of eaves of Japanese temples. When it was removed the smoke rose freely up the chimney. Under the stove was a dolly with casters for moving it. The cook's bench was in front of that. Firewood, including kindling, was piled up to the left of the stove. In the upper left corner of the cooking "hut" was a cupboard that was divided off for storing food that might spoil due to dampness. In the upper right corner was a cupboard for storing sugar and seasonings. This cooking "hut" was kept near the prow of the ship because the powder magazine was at the stern and this had to be kept as far as possible from fire.

The ship's cook was from Holland. The English sailors called him "The Dutchman." He was said to have been in Nagasaki twice. One day he said to the Japanese in a scornful manner, "Your country's customs---ugh!" There were live ducks, chickens and turkeys on board ship which were stabbed to death and cooked. On Sundays two bottles of grape wine were set on the table. It was strong so people drank only a little at a time. Thus the bottles lasted for a week. When the bottles became empty the sailors tossed them in the sea. The Japanese could not understand why they would throw such beautiful bottles away.

Foreign ships had decorative bows merely for the sake of appearance. They were constructed separately from the rest of the ship. Sailors used this place to relieve themselves as it was the highest place on the deck and they were not likely to get splashed by the waves there. The captain and other high officers had special toilet arrangements.

Day after day they sailed east [?] and one day two small islands were sighted. Jirokichi was told that it was only a two day trip to Edo from those islands. Upon hearing this, he pleaded with the captain, "We really would like to go to those islands." Captain Sen refused saying, "That is impossible. This ship is carrying a full load of goods. If those Japanese devils act up, we will have to jettison the cargo in order to make the ship light enough to fight back."[2]

The drifters noted that the Englishmen they met on the ship had a gentle outward appearance and they were soft-spoken, but they were also truly brave. They heard that it was their government's policy to pay people of high rank twice what ordinary people make, so men would strive hard with mind and body to get to the top. Considering this, the Japanese could understand Captain Sen's stand on the issue of approaching Japanese shores.

One day a massive hump was sighted on the water. The sailors shouted out in alarm, "A reef! A reef!" Captains Sen and Carter came out on the deck but they didn't get excited. "In this area," they said, "there are no reefs. Look again." It turned out to be a whale. When it began spouting water the sailors agreed. Oysters could be seen adhering to the back of the giant beast.

On a special map the officers on the ship determined the degrees of latitude and longitude and could find their destinations in this way. The ship's course was entered in a big log book every day with graphite [pencil]. If they made a mistake, it could be erased neatly. This [eraser] was made from dried horse's lip. [This Koga found hard to believe.]

When it was thought they should be getting close to Kamchatka, Captain Carter looked through his binoculars and called out, "We have gone too many degrees north. Turn the ship around at once," he ordered his crew. Captain Sen confirmed it saying, "You are right. We have sailed too far north." Jirokichi realized then that it was a safer navigation policy to have two captains on board.

The voyage continued for 30 or 40 days [actually less than 30] and at the end of August they arrived at the port of Kamchatka [Petropavlovsk] on the east coast of the peninsula. This northern outpost was located at 53 N. latitude. Rain mixed with snow was falling accompanied by a strong west wind. The bitter cold chilled the Japanese to the bone after having been in the tropics for many months.

The strong wind and many islands in the bay made it difficult to maneuver the ship into the harbor. The area reminded Jirokichi of Uraga Bay in that mountains surrounded the harbor on three sides. It was about five cho wide but only deep enough for two-mast ships to anchor there. Inside the bay was Gavin [actually Petropavlovsk--gavan was the Russian word for "harbor"], the city where the government offices were. Back of the city loomed the towering Voirichansukaya Mountain [Avachinskaia, 2175 meters]. It was covered with snow all year round so mariners used it as a target when entering the harbor. On the left side of the harbor there was a military cemetery. On the right side was a sandy beach where small boats were lined up. Adjacent to the bay was the Awajinsuka area [maybe Avacha].

Near the harbor cannons were set up in two places. There were about ten cannons in front of the docks. Behind them was a jail and a bell tower. On the south coast, near the soldiers' graves, there were ten huge cannons, and above the cemetery the gunpowder was stored. Beside that place was the barracks for the guards. Cannons were also set up around the government headquarters.

The chief of the colony and interpreter at this time was an American-born man named Metteru. His official rank was under-secretary, but in the absence of the chief secretary he was acting head. Metteru told Jirokichi's party that they would be staying at the cavalrymen's barracks. Meanwhile he would send a messenger to Irkutsk to get orders as to how to handle their affair.

The barracks was a one-story building 14 or 15 ken long and 6 1/2 ken wide on the north side of the river. It was northwest of Mr. Metteru's home. There were many glass windows in the barracks and one entrance. Upon entering the building the hall branched off to the left and right to where the soldiers' bunks were lined up. The room where they slept had wooden floors. It was only about seven shaku deep so when the soldiers stretched out to sleep they nearly touched both walls. In the center of the room in about a two ken space there was a row of posts which were about eight sun square. Wooden crossbars with metal fittings were attached at the top and bottom to hold the rifles. The metal fittings were intended to secure them to the rack. Under the rack the heavy floor board was hollowed out and the gun stock fit in there. Gun after gun was lined up with a space of about one shaku five sun between them. In the middle of the space was a hook on which the soldier hung his dagger, ammunition case and other equipment. All the guns had bayonets attached on the side, some were folded under the rifle. Such an arrangement was on both sides of the crossbar.

At the end of the gun rack was a place to put the soldiers' caps. There were 200 or 300 lined up on a three-<u>ken</u> board.

For bedding the soldiers used deer or bear fur. In the morning it was rolled up and put under the bed.

For a long time the Japanese had been eating big meals with the Americans and the English, now suddenly they had to be satisfied with crude military mess. For breakfast they were given only a big round bun and tea. At noon and for the evening meal they had soup with a little meat or fish in it.

There was a brass samovar for making tea about one <u>shaku</u> two <u>sun</u> high. A copper tube eight or nine <u>sun</u> in diameter stood up in the middle of the pot. At the base was a fire to heat the water. When the hot water in the urn boiled briskly the tap at the base of the samovar was turned and hot water came out. It was poured over tea leaves in a small ceramic cup and drunk.

As to how they made the soup, first they put about three <u>sho</u> of water in a big iron kettle about three <u>shaku</u> wide. This was set on a clay stove. Next they washed thoroughly five or six salmon and put them in a pan with about two <u>sho</u> of rice. They added water and let it boil. After a while they picked up the fish by their tails and shook the meat off from the bones. The bones were thrown away and the meat was mixed in with the rice. After the mixture became mushy the cook dipped out each person's share with a copper ladle which had a handle over two <u>shaku</u> five <u>sun</u> long and a bowl over three <u>sun</u> in diameter. Each soldier had a shallow wooden bowl about one <u>shaku</u> wide with a bamboo hoop around it. They used wooden spoons with handles over three <u>sun</u> long and one <u>sun</u> five <u>bu</u> wide. The same bowl was used for long periods of time so some had become caked with bloody flesh and a bad smell had permeated the wood.

The bread was different from American-style bread. The Americans poked holes in the top of the buns and put dates, grapes, currants, etc. in them before they were baked.

Their bread was soft and delicious, but the Japanese thought the Russian bread was very inferior. The grain was sent from Irkutsk and was of poor quality. For shipping it was packed tightly in a leather bag over two shaku wide. A bag of grain weighed as much as 12 kamme. When it reached Kamchatka the grain was sifted to separate the rough and rotten grains but then it was mixed with the husks and needle-like beards. To this coarse flour, barley dregs and vinegar were added before the bread was baked. (This fermented ingredient had a tinge of acidity and was really not vinegar). The loaves were shaped like Chinese manju [rounded on top] about one shaku in diameter and four sun thick and were baked. It became like a big mochi [rice cake]. Each loaf was divided into ten pieces and each soldier was given one slice. Eating this bread that was made from flour mixed with hard wheat beards was utterly like chewing on wood chips. The drifters said that their teeth could not cut through it and chewing on it made their gums bleed. They finally decided to only eat the soup while enduring the rancid odor of the soup bowls.

Each person was allotted a cube of beef about three sun four bu square each day which was boiled in the big iron kettle. The Japanese ate it but still they were always hungry. They finally became so perplexed about the food that they complained to Mr. Metteru. He said, "This is a very remote place and for that reason the soldiers are accustomed to a poor diet. I know the American and English food was delicious but here you cannot get such food at all. We knew when you came that you probably would not like the food. From now on, it may be better if you come to my home sometimes. Anyway, I will try to arrange better accommodations for you.

The Japanese party was then divided up and they acted as servants in Mr. Metteru's home and in the houses of two wealthy merchants. At last they had peace of mind as far as food was concerned, the meals they had there were not inferior to American and English cooking.

Three small rivers flowed through the city. The source of the river flowing from the north was a five or six cho swamp. Cattle grazed in the vicinity of the swamp.

Occasionally the cows would wander off toward the mountains and get killed by bears. The Japanese sometimes saw cows with scars from being clawed by bears. Northeast of the city there was a wide plain where vegetation grew thick. The land gradually rose up toward the foothills. The houses where the drifters lived were in the southeastern part of the city.

The Japanese enjoyed watching the soldiers' drills every day. They were similar to what they had seen in the Sandwich Islands but here the units faced each other, whereas in the Islands the soldiers lined up facing the commanding officer. The Japanese sometimes took part in the maneuvers on the grounds of the barracks. The Russians were very strict about keeping in step. If anyone was out of step, the drill officer would grab the soldier by his beard and yank him this way and that while giving him a severe scolding.

As for their uniforms, the officers wore a tunic called a gotsu [coat?] which hung down in back like a tail. Ordinary soldiers' coats had no tail. In summer they wore white trousers and in winter they had black ones. High officials had epaulettes made of twisted gold cord. The size was in proportion to their rank. They carried a sword, and a container of ammunition was affixed to their belts. Instead of epaulettes, ordinary soldiers had a woolen strip of yellow or red cloth about three sun long and two sun wide attached to their collars. There were two kinds of caps. Those who wore tall red caps were under the direct command of the Emperor. Their trousers had one colored stripe down the side. Those officers under the control of the base commander wore flat grey caps.

High officers, regardless of age, carried a cane. Some carried splendid ones made of ivory or bone. Long-term soldiers also used canes, but if commoners used them they would be looked upon with scorn and people would make sarcastic remarks like, "That's a suitable cane for you, isn't it?"

When Jirokichi was strolling along the coast by the wharves one day he saw some local people struggling to lift and carry rice bags to the warehouse. As he looked on, he couldn't help but want to help them out. When he picked up and carried a couple of the 16 <u>kamme</u> bags at one time, the people looked at him in astonishment. When the news of this remarkable feat reached the head of the province, Jirokichi was called before him to demonstrate his strength. As he showed the chief magistrate how much weight he could lift, the official looked over at his servants and said, "Is there anyone of you who can carry two bags at one time?"

"No one," they replied.

After that, Jirokichi showed them that he could even lift three bags at once.

Russian men liked to wrestle and sometimes Jirokichi wrestled sumo-style with them. They had much bigger physiques so he had to raise his head to look in their faces. They were not very skillful. Jirokichi dodged left and right as they lunged toward him and he could easily overturn them. The onlookers cheered and yelled, "You can't beat the Japanese!", while admiring Jirokichi's muscular strength. (Jirokichi had once taken part in a weight-lifting competition in Osaka and received a prize of a keg of sake for lifting an iron anchor weighing 72 <u>kamme</u>.)

Hachizaemon was the only servant in the home of the interpreter, Mr. Metteru. He and his wife had 16 children. The interpreter not only supported Hachizaemon, but he found employment for all the other drifters as well. Jirokichi worked in the home of a dry goods merchant named Peyajimishiko [phonetic spelling] who had an aged mother and a 17 or 18-year old manservant living with him.[3] Jirokichi stayed there only 40 or 50 days and then served in the new Governor's home. Tasaburo and Rokubei worked for someone named Karumakofu [phonetic spelling]. Tasaburo and Rokubei did not get along well, so Rokubei was shifted to the home of a person named Vuchirashi [phonetic spelling], who was an official recorder. Besides the master and his wife, there was another couple living there. They each had two children. During the time that Rokubei was there one of the daughters got married. Rokubei thought it was strange that when she moved in with her new family she took only one small bag like a toilet case with her.

One time Rokubei was asked to go into the mountains with a dog sled to get firewood. He drove the dogs to the mountains but then they would not follow his orders at all. The lead dog returned home and the others followed. Rokubei was at a loss as to what to do.

Kinzo served a subordinate official named Kazaka [phonetic spelling]. There was only one couple and no other servants. His duties were to chop wood and carry water. The couple was not very kind to him so he refused to stay there more than one month. Then he shifted to Captain Nikolai's house where there was a couple and an infant daughter. They had one other manservant. It was very quiet and gloomy. Kinzo was expected to do only the laundry. It was not at all interesting so after two or three months he moved again and then worked for someone named Hichapan Nikolai [phonetic spelling]. There were a couple, their children and some servants. Kinzo did not like the way he was treated there either and he reported it to the interpreter. Rokubei had left Karumakofuku's place so Kinzo was asked to replace him there. At this place there were the parents, two sons and three daughters. For servants there was an old couple, their son and his wife and their two children. Perhaps having Tasaburo and Kinzo there too only added to their burden. In this house the two Japanese alternated working day and night. During the night they acted as watchmen of the storehouse. They kept a big dog which was kept in a small house during the day, and at night a rope was tied around its neck and connected to a ring on a rope that extended from the roof of the house to the eaves of the storehouse. This enabled the dog to run back and forth between them. The dog would bark sharply as the man on watch walked around using wooden clappers to ward off thieves.

In this place servants were engaged by the order of the government according to specific regulations. They had to get official approval if they wanted to change jobs, but the Japanese were given special treatment. There didn't seem to be any hurt feelings if they left one employer for another.

When they met a former master on the road he was friendly and said something like, "Come again and visit." Wherever they went and whatever they did, the Japanese did not receive any wages.

About a month after the drifters arrived in Kamchatka the newly-appointed governor arrived. The Japanese joined the people who went out to greet him on his arrival from Irkutsk. After that Jirokichi served in Governor Nikolai Nikarauchi's home. His residence was located on a fairly high place in the center of the city. Facing east, the house was surrounded by a simple fence and had a roofed gate. Diagonally across was an 80-<u>ken</u> vegetable garden. To the left of the house was the hospital and behind it was the bathhouse. On the right was the church.

The governor often had parties to which Jirokichi was invited. Everyone dressed beautifully on these occasions. An American had presented Jirokichi with some fine clothes including some red silk shirts which he frequently wore.

One time the governor went for a long ride in the suburbs. A guide led the procession on horseback, two subordinate officials followed, and the governor followed them. Jirokichi rode along as one of the attendants.

Jirokichi served as an attendant to the governor's son one time when he went to spear salmon. He carried a spear about two <u>ken</u> long with a sharp hook on the end. Over one shoulder he slung a creel made of woven grass. It had an opening about two <u>shaku</u> in diameter and was about one <u>shaku</u> five <u>sun</u> deep. They went to a creek not far from the city that was about two <u>ken</u> wide. The thick ice had begun to melt and the salmon huddled up to the roots of trees that grew along the banks. He stood on the bank and threw the spear. This was such a cold place that the salmon were rather thin and not so delicious.

At the year's end in accordance with regulations regarding his new appointment, the governor went on a personal inspection tour to the southern part of the peninsula to observe the life of the native Kamichidari [Kamchadals].

His wife, Maria Aleksandrovna, and their five or six-year old son accompanied them riding in a dog sled. Jirokichi, along with the stewards, were given the responsibility of taking care of the official residence. But unfortunately the servants acted as if, "When the cat's away, the mice will play," for they fooled around with the precious gold, silver and pearl belongings of the governor. There were eating utensils made of pure gold, their handles and the blades of the knives weighed as much as 70 momme, the spoons were 15 or 16 momme and the forks were a little less than the spoons. The servants sneaked them out of the cupboards and tinkered with them as well as with the furniture. They also played with the wife's harp, an organ and with the tea service.

Unexpectedly Maria Aleksandrovna returned one day earlier than planned. The furniture and utensils were scattered here and there all over the house. The stewards had gone out somewhere and Jirokichi was left alone in the house. He scurried about trying to tidy up before going out to greet her. One by one the servants rushed back home. The wife did not say anything or scold anyone. The next day the governor returned. When he heard the particulars about what happened in their absence he thanked Jirokichi, but he harshly scolded the servants. Before long two of them were sent away to the Kamichidari area. The stewards were told to serve as guards at the prison for seven days.

One of the governor's maids, Kiniya, was a charming and pretty 18-year old girl who had been brought out from the capital. Many times the governor said to Jirokichi, "How about it? I'll ask that girl to be your bride. We can all go to Petrograd together some day." He told the Japanese that the Imperial Capital was a big city over 70 ri square, far from this desolate place.

In November or December [actually spring--Easter] the Japanese realized there was a week set aside for worshipping God when it was their custom to abstain from eating bread and butter. People went around begging for repentance of everybody. "Please forgive me for any wrongdoing I have done," they said when they greeted people. Everybody did it regardless of rank--there was no distinction between the rich and poor or men and women.

On the first day of the observance Jirokichi woke up to the sound of many people coming and going. He thought it was very strange, and to add to his confusion the servants in the house began coming to his bedside and kissing him while begging his pardon for their sins.

As a Japanese he was not accustomed to the custom of kissing and was repelled by the familiarity of it, so he always kept his mouth tightly closed when Russians greeted him in this way. It was especially repulsive for him to be kissed by a man with a beard.

In March or April a strong earthquake shook the area of Kamchatka. Three ships that were anchored in the harbor at the time were washed ashore. Rokubei said that when he tried to run out of the house he was held back by the Russians. Several houses were destroyed in the quake and it caused some fires. Ashes from a nearby volcano covered much of the land including the beaches.

Shortly after arriving in Kamchatka, Shichizaemon was bothered with pain and swelling in his scrotum. Some of the other sailors teased him and accused him of fooling around with women. After landing, his condition became worse so they all accompanied him to see a doctor. The doctor seemed to be man in his forties and was dressed in ordinary clothes. For the medical examination the doctor first took Shichizaemon's pulse, then examined his eyes and tongue. He felt his stomach and discreetly examined the diseased area. He diagnosed his trouble as being paki or chancres. The doctor decided that the Japanese should be hospitalized.

Upon entering the hospital Shichizaemon was given a pillow and his bedding by the administrator. Attended by two nurses, the doctor cut away the diseased part. Every day the patient was given two bags of herbal medicine which one of the nurses boiled for him. Besides the herbs, he had to take a pill each day, and salve was applied to the infected area. His food was always weighed before it was served to him. Every morning at about 10 o'clock the doctor came to his room to examine him. When he was in the hospital there were 40 or 50 other patients there as well.

When Shichizaemon was undergoing treatment in the hospital one of the male nurses did not sterilize the instruments or cleanse the wound properly and then refused to own up to the oversight. What is more, when he was summoned for questioning he ran away. He was later apprehended and brought before a group of one hundred of his fellow workers and was punished by whipping.

On this occasion the Japanese said the punishment commenced with the signal of the beating of a drum. The accused was stripped to the waist and was flogged as he moved from one person to another standing in a semi-circle. Tasaburo, Rokubei and Jirokichi, who witnessed the beating, heard that he had been sentenced to 500 lashes but after making two rounds, the man fainted and had to be carried to the hospital for treatment.[4]

Well, in January [1841] Shichizaemon again suffered excruciating pain and he had to walk with a cane. By March he needed two canes. Finally he could not stand up at all and was like an invalid. The diseased part, however, seemed to have gotten better. His fellow sailors squeezed out radish juice and made a compress with it to apply to the painful area. The diseased places were sometimes cut away with scissors.

When the Japanese heard that they would be taken to Okhotsk on the east coast of Siberia in June, Shichizaemon was not able to join them. The doctor advised him to postpone the departure. He ended up sailing on another ship twenty days after the others left Kamchatka. He had fully recovered by then.

Chapter VII

OKHOTSK

Thousands of wedding lamps
The darkness turns to daylight.

In June [1841] according to the Russian calendar, two
ships with two masts came into the harbor from Okhotsk. One
was named <u>Tarankosuka</u> [phonetic spelling]. The captain wore
gold epaulettes. The other ship was the <u>Nikolai</u>, commanded
by Captain Nikolai Mitautorusu [phonetic spelling] whose
epaulettes were silver.

During their ten-month stay in Kamchatka the drifters
were always hoping that an order would come from the
capital for their repatriation, but it did not come. They were
not given any explanation as to why they were to go to
Okhotsk on one of these ships, but they did hear that
communications with the capital were better there. The five
Japanese, excluding Shichizaemon, then boarded ship once
again. The ship was loaded with fox and badger pelts.
Before he left the governor's home, Jirokichi was offered
clothes. He courteously declined saying, "I was given many
clothes by the Americans and the English." The governor
seemed impressed by his lack of greed.

After sailing only three or four <u>ri</u> from the harbor the
captain of the ship realized that the documents related to the
Japanese sailors had been left behind. The ship was turned
back towards Petropavlovsk and blank shots were fired as a
signal. Cannons went off three or four times, their booms
reverberating from one mountain to the other. The captain
said, "Using one of our lifeboats would be faster than a
barge." In a short time some men in a rowboat got the
documents and came back. Then again the cannons roared as
a signal of thanks. Jirokichi thought that they used some
prearranged code. For short distances of three to five <u>cho</u>

they used a megaphone, but when signalling from distances over one ri they communicated with cannons.

After the ship had proceeded about 50 ri the sails received a crosswind and the ship took a southwestward course. In 14 or 15 days they sailed between Kamchatka's Cape Lopatka and Horomutsuri [phonetic spelling-Paramushir?] Island. These straits were barely two ri wide and were considered very dangerous by navigators of big ships. When they succeeded in sailing through the passage safely a celebration party was usually held on board ship. After that it was still a five-day voyage to the mainland.

At one point when the cape was still clearly visible to the east a weight was let down and the depth was determined to be 30 fathoms. When the weight was brought up marine plants adhered to it. After continuing for about one ri the weight was dropped again. This time the depth was 150 fathoms and only mud stuck to the weight. Three days later the mountains of Okhotsk came into view. Near the offing there was a huge iceberg.

In early July the ship entered the mouth of the Okhotsk River in the afternoon. About 20 local citizens stood on the shore greeting its arrival. The ship was pulled with a tow rope and by some mistake it hit a shoal. At that time it was low tide and the ship began to list. Everyone ran about in confusion and unloaded the cargo. When the ship became lighter it could anchor at the "Company" docks.[1]

The next day Jirokichi's party went ashore and walked along the shore toward the city. On the way there were grain elevators. When they passed near them the soldier on guard duty suddenly stood at attention. The Japanese thought it was strange and muttered to each other, "Do you suppose he is always in dead earnest like that? Just because we walk by, he doesn't have to flaunt his authority," and laughed about it together.

First the Japanese were taken to the office of the governor at the branch office of the Company. This was a separate house---like a storehouse. There were no other residences there, it was simply called the "Company". Cannons were set up in five or six places around the Company office. They were the biggest cannons the Japanese had seen so far. The drifters were told that a runner had set out for the capital to find out what to do about their situation.

Okhotsk was the eastern terminus of the crossing of the great land mass of Russia from Petrograd. The city was located on the Kufutoikawa [phonetic spelling] River, which was about three <u>cho</u> wide with a depth of about two <u>cho</u>. The river bed was stony with sand bars here and there. The shapes of the latter constantly changed as the volume of water varied with the tides. The mouth of the river was only about one <u>cho</u> wide, so only two-mast ships could enter.

The houses of the city residents were lined up on the north side of the river facing upstream. The row of houses was orderly with no vacant lots between them. Near these houses were the traders' storehouses. At night they were locked up and the employees returned to their homes. South of the storehouses cannons were set up on platforms along the river side. At the water's edge there were many small boats. These were not dugout canoes but conventional boats made with nails. There was a watchtower in the area where guards remained on duty day and night.[2]

At the time the Japanese were there a ship was being built at the shipyard. The methods for pulling up big ships into drydock and for launching them were similar to what they had seen in the Sandwich Islands. There was a hospital, barracks, a church, a men's prison and a separate prison for women. About 1 <u>ri</u> northwest of the city there was a graveyard.

On the opposite shore of the river were the crude dwellings of the Tingalese people. Because they lived by fishing they moved from place to place, so their houses were simple teepee style made by setting up wooden poles tied at the top and spread out at the base. The poles were covered with straw matting.

The Russian-American Company wharf was about   ri downstream from the city where the river flowed into the sea. The officers had been sent to this post from Irkutsk. Military preparations were strongest for the Company, the city's defenses were second.   In front of their building on the seashore ten cannons were set up here and there. The harbor faced the sea so three-mast ships were anchored here.

The Japanese were again asked to be servants. In this place they worked at the governor's home. His residence was a two-story wooden building surrounded by a fence. The gate opened on the north side.   In the yard there was a large greenhouse covered with translucent paper for growing vegetables. On the west side of the residence there were some 20 cannons lined up. The road in front was covered with gravel so when walking barefoot one's feet did not get dirty.

The governor of Okhotsk, Nikolai Vokoroshi [Golovnin], had come here three years before to serve a seven-year term of office.[3]   The lieutenant governor was an old man over 60 named Petr Ivanich. Long ago he served as an officer to Commander Rikord [on the Diana] when Takadaya Kahei was captured.[4]   Because of this connection with the Japanese, Jirokichi's party often visited his house and received special favors.

During their stay in Okhotsk the drifters were once shown a portrait of Takadaya Kahei. He was dressed in a kimono with a fine silk haori [coat] and wore a sword at his hip. The Russians still loved and respected him as an onjin [benevolent person].

The governor was fond of bonsai [potted plants?] which he had arranged on shelves in his office. The shelves were about six shaku high and each shelf was about four shaku square. The trees and plants were all in wooden boxes not in porcelain pots.

Fruits and vegetables were very precious in this northern extremity. Various kinds of melons and vegetables were raised inside of small huts. These huts were about three ken wide, seven or eight ken long and about six shaku high.

hinges on one side of the top so it could be opened on sunny days. Rich soil was put inside where the seeds were planted. Sometimes the young plants were transplanted outside. Cucumbers grew very big in these hothouses. They experimented with watermelons but they were small and not tasty. Two or three kinds of flowers, including pinks, were also raised in these huts.[5]

In Russia there ware two varieties of cabbage. One was called takeppe. This was common in the Sandwich Islands, too. The stalk grew to about three shaku tall. The leaves were thick and tough and coated with a white powder so they were not suitable for eating. The other was called kapashita [phonetic spellings]. It looked just like a large peony bud. When it was cut in half, one could see the pink leaves packed firmly. The outer leaves were three sun wide and about five sun long. When pickled they were delicious.

The radishes were shaped like the Japanese daikon [a large white radish] but they were more slender. They were grainy and tough so they didn't boil them for eating but shaved off the thin skin, put salt on them, and served them with alcoholic beverages. The carrots, onions and turnips were similar to those in Japan. Beets were red, three or four sun in diameter and shaped like turnips. They were sweet when boiled with seasonings.

Kapposuta [phonetic spelling] was a kind of greens. They were put in a tub, pickled in salt, and served with beef stock or some rice. At this place they could not have fresh vegetables from October to June, so this kapposuta was very useful. They also had potatoes that could be stored all through the winter.

In this vicinity officials came to help the local people experiment in raising barley. They succeeded in growing healthy stalks and leaves but there was no grain at all. At the time when they planted the seeds a priest attended and read prayers. The Japanese assumed it was a kind of charm.

Five people were serving in the governor's home while the Japanese were there. Among them, two lived in and the

Five people were serving in the governor's home while the Japanese were there. Among them, two lived in and the others returned to their own homes at about 8 p.m. One of those who lived at the house was named Nikolai Hiyodori [phonetic spelling] who was on kitchen duty. He believed in some special religion in which liquor and tobacco were banned. He was not married. This religion also dictated the removal of one's sexual organs. At the governor's residence there was a bathroom in a separate building. Every seven days water was prepared for the servants' baths. One time when the Japanese were there Hiyodori came in with a male friend who belonged to the same faith. They were embarrassed lest the Japanese see their bodies, so they put the lantern outside. This Hiyodori had a weak constitution. He could not lift even a five-<u>kamme</u> weight. It was said that when he urinated he used a wooden pipe. The woman who joined that religion had to have their breasts removed. In that case they inserted some artificial device in the shape of a sphere.

As for Russian marriages, first the two families had a meeting to make a tentative agreement. Then a matchmaker was chosen and they selected a lucky day for the wedding. On the morning of the wedding day the bride and groom dressed up beautifully and walked hand in hand to the church. If it was an evening ceremony, the road was brightly lit with many lanterns making it seem like mid-day. These lanterns were put up by poor people hoping for monetary handouts from the groom after the ceremony.

A priest dressed in elaborate vestments was waiting at the church when the couple arrived. Inside the church thousands of candles were burned making it like daylight there, too. The bride and groom walked hand in hand behind the priest to the altar where they exchanged kisses several times. Then they each kissed the icon two or three times. All the time the ceremony was in progress villagers gathered around outside the church, sometimes peeping in the windows. They talked and laughed as they discussed whether the ritual was performed skillfully or not.

After the priest read from the Bible the newlyweds left the church and returned home where guests thronged about congratulating the couple. A magnificent banquet was served and music was played. The drinking, singing and partying continued for as long as a week.

One time Tasaburo and Jirokichi had a quarrel which ended in a fist fight. Jirokichi knocked him down and he passed out. As a result Jirokichi was scolded by the governor and told to live in the soldiers' barracks for thirty days. He could not go outside during that time, but later he could return to the governor's home.[6]

Hunters in Russia sometimes used a howitzer type of gun. The double-barreled rifle was mounted on a stand and when not in use the legs of the stand were folded up and were joined to the gun barrel. When they were about to shoot they set up the mount, rested the gun on it, aimed and fired. The fact that it was double-barreled proved useful when the animal was startled by the sound of the first shot. There was also a sword attached to the end of the rifle in case of an emergency. If the hunter was in any immediate danger of attack, he also had a sword on his hip to use. When discharging the gun, the firer used a detonator.

When hunters saw flocks of birds they could kill as many as fifty with one shot. The birds were very nimble, so at the sound of a gun they instantly dove in the water but Russian hunters took this into consideration beforehand and aimed at the water.

There were brilliantly feathered birds in Siberia that were no bigger than a cicada. Russian people shot and then stuffed them for gifts to be sent to the imperial capital. There was said to be a big museum at the royal capital where various flora and fauna from all over the various domains were exhibited. Russian territory was so vast that it would have been impossible for the Emperor to visit every area, so at this museum he could examine them as an aid in determining national policy.

Sleds were drawn by reindeer as well as dogs in Siberia. These reindeer were larger than ordinary deer. One day the Japanese were shown a huge animal horn. It was slightly curved and over six shaku long. The outer surface was black but it was white underneath. They were told that it was from a mammoth.

Okhotsk got less snow than Kamchatka but the Russians here, as well as everywhere else, enjoyed winter sports. They built a long wooden slide from the roof of a big building to the ground and this was covered with snow. The snow was well-trampled and made slippery before boys and girls coasted down on their sleds. Some skillful ones would stand up on the sleds and go down smoothly. Others would lie down on the sleds. The girls were not so good at it and as they went down their skirts flew up over their heads and everyone laughed. Even Maria, the governor's wife, would go sledding. The servants pushed her sled on the ice rink.

One time Maria invited the Japanese to attend a party at the governor's home. Everyone drank and danced and had a very good time. They were repeatedly encouraged to dance but the drifters declined because they didn't know how to do the steps. But since they kept on insisting Hachizaemon finally sang and Kinzo and Tasaburo showed the Russians how the bon odori was done. Everybody was pleased and the shipmates were given some silver coins by the governor's wife.

The people in Okhotsk drank vodka that had been shipped from Irkutsk in big wooden casks. While brewing vodka they added chopped clove leaves. The aroma was delicious and it was piquant to the tongue. Even though the vodka was usually diluted with water it was still very strong.

Russians also took snuff at parties. The powdered tobacco used for sniffing was kept in a small box with a cover on it. When using it they picked up a pinch between their thumb and forefinger and rubbed it with the saliva in their upper and lower gums. They sometimes inhaled it through the nose. The first time a person tried it they usually sneezed a lot. One time a fellow said to Jirokichi at a party, "The way you people smoke with a kiseru pipe is bad for the health. What do you think about our snuff?" Women and children in Russia did not use tobacco but old women sometimes relaxed by using snuff. Russian men liked to smoke by the light of a fire. During the day they used candles for light so they did not need a tobacco tray. On the ship too, they smoked while sitting around a big lamp.

When a Russian had a dinner party everyone sat around a big long table covered with a white cloth. Each guest was given a knife, fork and spoon. The cook polished the silverware every day so they sparkled and shone. Various kinds of wine were served, some weak and some strong. There were as many as ten bottles on the table at one time. The host and guests chose whatever kind they wanted and poured it themselves. Pouring it for others was not common among Westerners [a practice always observed in Japan]. One time the governor said to the drifters, "If Japanese are not served, they don't drink," as he filled their glasses to the brim. The Western custom was to pour oneself a glassful, gulp it down in one swig, then turn the glass over and shake out the last drop.

Peshika [phonetic spelling] was chess in Russian. There were 64 squares in eight rows horizontally and vertically on the board. Alternate squares were painted black and white. Each player had eight chessmen which were in the shape of old sages carved with ivory. The pieces could be moved only on the black squares. If they were in the adversary's territory the men could be moved freely diagonally. In this way, they could advance or retreat while taking the enemy's pawns. If two were lined up in a row, they could not capture them, however.

Since there were fewer squares on the board than in Japanese shogi [chess], Jirokichi thought that it might be a simpler game, but no matter how many times he played, he could not win. The Russians could read their adversary's moves ten or twenty times in advance. Sometimes the Russians played for money.

The drifters were shown a picture of an airship in Okhotsk. There was also an illustration of a man being shot from a cannon. The cannon was short and thick, shaped like a mortar. The man held on to a huge umbrella, and when he was shot up in the air he opened it so that he could descend slowly to the ground. When the wind was strong he could be flown over six <u>ri</u>, but this was exceedingly risky. To lessen the danger of getting hurt they usually did it on a day when there was no wind. In that case he landed about three <u>ri</u> from where he was shot out of the cannon.

The governor had a villa about 1 <u>ri</u> northwest of the city. On Sundays the Japanese went there to enjoy themselves and wait on the governor's wife. Nearby in the wilderness black mushrooms and wild strawberries were abundant. The juice of the wild strawberries, as well as grape juice, was kept in a storehouse. Maria would let the sailors dip out the juice sometimes with a spoon and drink it.

One time when the Japanese were at the villa Maria's father, Petovuna, and her younger brother, Petrovina, were also spending some time there. This brother acted as the governor's recording secretary. At that time the governor told the drifters the following story:

> In fact, I am Golovnin's nephew. On one occasion when my uncle was in Japan he received an inexpressibly great kindness and I, myself, feel deep appreciation for that. I have always wanted to return that favor, as a matter of fact, it has been on my mind day and night. When I unexpectedly heard about you being in the vicinity, I thought it was a blessing from heaven.

Jirkokichi's party realized then that it was because of this, that the governor was especially hospitable to them. They even ate their meals with him. But none of the drifters knew about the incident in 1811 in which Golovnin was captured and imprisoned by the Japanese. The governor explained to them that his uncle had written a book giving the details of the experience. The governor kept the book hidden away so people wouldn't see it, or hear about it, but the Japanese asked the lieutenant governor to read the book to them. It told of the imprisonment of the high naval officer for three years and the great hardships he experienced. For one day and night he was given no food at all, then a Japanese man secretly slipped a rice ball to him. He was extremely thankful for this great blessing. His captors at first tempted him and he was caught by using flattery. Later he tried to escape into the mountains but was soon recaptured. Then he received terrible contempt and insults. Such things the lieutenant governor interpreted from Golovnin's record entitled, "Memoirs of Captivity in Japan."

As Jirokichi's party listened to this story all the color drained from their faces from shock. They were so deeply affected by the details that they could do nothing but weep. Finally they said to the lieutenant governor, "Then as for the Russian people, Japan is thought of as a real enemy. But we have been given a warm welcome. We are thankful for Russia's tolerant national policy and for the governor's benevolent heart."

Another day the governor said to the Japanese, "You have no relation to the Golovnin incident." He did not seem to harbor any bitterness and added, "It was an act of the Japanese shogunate government. You are merely sailors, so you need not take any responsibility for such an action."[7]

Russian people sometimes said to Jirokichi, "You people had better not return home. Why don't you settle down here? In this place a person in difficult financial circumstances has only to turn his cap inside out and hold it out while standing by the roadside. Everybody would sympathize and donate money, and soon the cap would be filled with gold. Also poor people can receive welfare payments from the government. After the Muroran incident the Golovnin party was taken prisoner. When they eventually returned home they received cordial mercy from the Emperor and could live out their lives in comfort. In Japan do they have such a benevolent practice?" In this way they questioned Jirokichi who was burning with desire to get back home. He could only smile and say, "I don't know."

The Muroran incident referred to a dispute that broke out when some Russians came ashore in Ezo. An old man of about 70 said to Jirokichi, "I was with many sailors who came to this mountain (the Russians thought that 'Muroran' was the name of a mountain) to cut down some trees. Some Japanese people hidden in the grass suddenly shot at us and one of the sailors was killed. We were so surprised we threw our axes down and ran back to the ship. We sailed away until the top of the mast could no longer be seen from shore and sought safety in the offing. We discussed how to retaliate and decided to put ashore again under cover of darkness carrying a cannon to the top of an adjacent mountain. From there we aimed at the guardpost. As soon as the first cannon shot rang out the guards dispersed like fallen leaves and fled the scene."[8]

In the governor's home there was a big stove about ten <u>shaku</u> high in the middle of the room to provide heat. The stovepipe extended through the ceiling to the second floor and there was a chimney above that. In some places a furnace was set up with pipe extensions that heated four adjoining rooms. There were also stoves for heating three rooms at once.

Every morning a manservant brought in two bundles of firewood. When the logs were almost burned the damper in the chimney was removed. Than the ashes were put over the logs and they would continue to smolder for a long time. A thermometer hung on the wall so they could control the temperature, always keeping it like mid-autumn. When snow piled up as high as the eaves the residents still did not have to wear more than one linen garment in the house. If it got too warm, the damper was closed on the stovepipe and a window was opened. Outside the window was a fan that blew in fresh air. Then when the temperature dropped to autumn temperatures the window was closed.

In high-class homes they kept lamps burning day and night. The oil used in the lamps had a light blue tinge and gave off an unpleasant odor. They called this oil "kerego of Koroa" [musk?] saying it was made from the brains of a cow. When going out for the evening men and women dabbed it on their faces. It was also applied to the collar of woolen clothes, so even if they were dirty they gave off this fragrance.

The toilet at the magistrate's home was fitted out with beautiful brocade cloth. One sat on a four-shaku square platform over an opening five or six sun in diameter which was lined with padded brocade. No bad odors were emitted because there was no open space. In front of the place where one sat there was a tobacco tray, spittoon, censer, etc. for people who wanted to relax there.

During the winter the walls would freeze, so in order to get water the servants would have to make holes in the ice on the river, pump out the water, and carry it back on the dog sled. One time an accident occurred in which the sled fell in the icy water.

Besides the Tingalese [?] tribe of natives there were tribes called Koriyaka [Koriaks] and Tsungasu [Tungus]. They ware said to be very barbaric. Their facial expressions were ferocious and their cheek bones stuck out so much that their faces were almost triangular. Their lips were terribly thick. The Japanese were told that they had no pubic hair and the truth was borne out when they saw some of the naked tribesmen fishing for salmon in the river one day.

Sometimes the drifters saw Tingalese men and women coming to the city to exchange sable pelts for gunpowder. After examining the pelts the soldiers would take a certain amount of gunpowder from a wooden bucket and weigh it. The Tingalese woman wore leather dresses heavily decorated with precious stones.

There were separate prisons for men and women in Russia located far apart. Soldiers stood guard at the gates. Women were given severe punishment for committing adultery, and girls under 17 who had had intimate relations with men were sent to prison. When it came to light that a maid in the home of a non-commissioned officer was having an affair with an official who had come out from Petrograd she was sentenced to a flogging. After that wound was healed she had to spend ten days in prison before she could go back to work.

Sometimes the drifters saw people whose noses had been cut off or partially removed. When Kinzo asked the interpreter about that he was told that in Petrograd they cut off the noses of criminals. Those that the Japanese saw had been banished to this area. Others had their genital organs cut off, or they were branded for life with tell-tale letters on their foreheads.

Army deserters were harshly punished according to Russian criminal law. The Japanese witnessed a military flogging in Okhotsk. The commanding officer and the second in command stood at the head of two lines of fifty soldiers each. Each soldier was holding a bundle of willow twigs. After the statement of offense was read, the deserter was led down between the lines by soldiers holding on to each of his arms. One after the other, the soldiers hit him on the buttocks with the switch. If he had been sentenced to 100 lashes, he was led through the ranks one time. Sometimes the penalty was two or three times or even over five times.

Jirokichi saw a soldier who had been sentenced to 500 lashes. When he had been hit 20 or 30 times he slumped over in agony. When the flogging was over his buttocks were reduced to a pulp. Jirokichi said he couldn't bear to look at the pathetic sight.

The offenders were taken to a hospital right after the whippings were over. They usually recovered in about ten days and then they went back to work. Jirokichi could hardly believe it was possible, so one soldier let down his pants and showed him his injury. Only a black and blue bruise remained. Their medical treatment was so effective that a scab formed over the wound within a week making it possible to recover in a short time.

According to the drifters, foreigners referred to their countryman as "Japanese devils." Then they added, "Only in Japan and China were people punished by decapitation. It is not seen in other countries as it is such a cruel custom." Instead of capital punishment, in many countries it was common to attach both ends of a heavy iron chain to both ankles of the criminal. That chain was over eight <u>bu</u> thick and it weighed over five <u>kamme</u>, so he could not get away. He was taken to a blacksmith to have it welded to his legs so it could not be removed. The chain was long enough so the criminal could pull it up from between his legs and over his head thus making it possible to move around. The men who received this punishment received from the official headquarters money for his evening meal every day which amounted to the equivalent of five five-<u>sen</u> coins. He was expected to carry out various duties for his keep, however. He was not allowed to live with his wife or family.

One building served as the hospital in Okhotsk. Many people could be hospitalized at the same time in rooms lined up on both sides of the central corridor. There was a nurse for each patient and a medical student assisted them. Doctors made the rounds twice a day. Medicine, food and bedding were supplied by the hospital. Officials and high-class people did not enter the hospital, but ordinary soldiers did. At one time Jirokichi was admitted to the hospital for treatment, so he could observe the circumstances.

Jirokichi saw treatment for a malignant tumor on the back of a patient's hand. As in the operation in the Sandwich Islands, the patient was first tied down tightly with leather straps so he felt little pain. Then the flesh was scraped off. In this case the afflicted part was not at the joint so the bone did not have to be cut with a saw. The surgeons found out that the poison had spread to the shoulder and back, so the patient could not be saved.

When operating on a patient with a bone-decaying disease the surgeon inserted an iron tube about as thick as a <u>saya</u> [sheathe for a calligraphy brush] in the infected part. The width of the tube tapered down at the end to make insertion easier and from the wider end the doctor could see the inflammation in detail. Then he inserted a knife which was curved on the end in order to scoop out the infected part. When the tube was removed, the incision was daubed with ointment and the area was wrapped in bandages. It did not take long before the patient was completely cured, Jirokichi was told.

There were two rather mysterious deaths while the drifters were staying in Okhotsk. One time when a cossack chief was returning to his home two or three ri out in the country, he suddenly died. The lieutenant governor, accompanied by a doctor, went there to investigate the death. The Japanese saw them take out a small brass scale with a ring about three bu wide attached. The ring was put around the dead man's head to find out if he was really wise or not [?]. It seemed that there were some suspicious circumstances surrounding the officer's death. Jirokichi heard that an autopsy would be conducted to find out if the man had been poisoned.

In another case a person committed suicide by drinking poison. His body was carried about one ri into the mountains where an autopsy was performed. This was usually done in the case of suicides in Russia.

When Lt. Governor Petr Ivanich died the Japanese could experience a high official's funeral. First a priest was summoned to offer prayers. After that, six men carried the coffin behind the priest in a procession. The funeral attendees followed along behind the coffin. At the church the local priest, along with the archbishop, removed the lid of the coffin and the corpse was displayed. Much to the surprise of the Japanese, he was dressed in very elaborate clothes with epaulettes as big as tea cups. The priest then delivered an address to the departing soul according to their faith and the church rites were over. Then the relatives and fellow officers filed past the coffin and kissed the deceased. Children and subordinate officers kissed his hand. When that was finished the lid was replaced on the coffin.

The widow, a young woman in her twenties, was the Lt. Governor's second wife. The Japanese said it was grievous to see her weep as she kissed her dead husband. Jirokichi remembered that moment after he returned to Japan. He said that he can still see the sadness in her eyes and share her grief for he, himself, felt close to the Lt. Governor and his family.

The coffin was carried out of the church and taken to the cemetery in the outskirts of the city. While the coffin was being lowered into the ground about fifty soldiers, who had led the procession to the grave, shouted something in unison while facing the east and then they fired their rifles many times. The sound of the gun shots resounded from the mountains like thunder. Branches were then laid criss-cross over the casket before the grave was filled with earth. On a later day a roofed hut was built over the grave.

High-class people had little huts over their graves but common people simply had their graves marked with a wooden cross shaped like the Japanese letter . If it decomposed, it was not replaced by a new one.

Russia and France believed in the same papal religion [according to the drifters] but in appearance they were very different. In Russia they had holy images cast in gold and silver which were three or four shaku tall.

As for Russian schools and education, children began school at about age six. They had various lessons each day including Bible-reading, penmanship, arithmetic, etc. The officers' children were taught war strategy and navigation starting in the first grade. In the latter lessons they made big models of ships. The teacher would get on the ships and teach the children how to hoist the sails, pull the ropes, etc. If the children were inattentive, even those of noble families were whipped on the buttocks with a willow switch. Jirokichi actually saw this done.

Jirokichi said that high-class Russians with a good education had a kind human nature and had only praise for Japanese things, but common people hurled insults at Japan. They would say things like, "Japan's government is terrible. They look upon foreign countries with unreasonable scorn. If we wanted to, we could send as many as 200 warships from our capital to blockade Japan. Moreover, we could easily take possession of Mutsu [the Tohoku area in northeastern Honshu] in three years by sending out fifty of our ships. But as long as Japan acts in the Japanese way and the government can keep the country peaceful, we cannot interfere." They went on to warn their Japanese guests, "If your country becomes even more obstinate, however, and continues to scorn us, we will show absolutely no mercy in conquering your country. Meanwhile, we will continue to be as patient as possible, but if and when the Japanese go beyond our limit of patience, we will go and make a conquest."

Also, Jirokichi heard a Russian make disparaging remarks about the Japanese Emperor saying, "That stupid one in Kyoto is perhaps a good-natured man, but the 'king' is the one in Edo." Another person said, "Japan is covered with a curtain. Soldiers are hiding behind it, but we can easily crush them."

When the runner who had gone to the capital returned at the end of June [1842] he brought orders that the Japanese sailors should be taken to Sitka in Alaska. It was explained that it would be easier to get on board a ship going toward northern Japan from there.

The governor explained to the drifters that they would be sailing on a ship that had recently come into Okhotsk harbor. They were told that four big ships regularly plied the route between Kamchatka and Okhotsk carrying supplies, but their schedules could not be disrupted for this kind of trip because they were so busy. Furthermore, they were often troubled with frozen seas. The Japanese were told that the harbor in Sitka did not freeze because of the range of volcanic mountains near by that had veins running down to the sea.

The governor boarded the ship [the drifters could not remember the name of the ship or the captain's name] with the Japanese and gave the orders to the captain. Then he said to the drifters, "As for your repatriation, first you must get on this captain's ship and go to Sitka." It was not until mid-July that the ship sailed.[9] While waiting for departure, the Japanese men walked around Okhotsk in the daytime and slept on the ship at night. As they bid farewell to the friends they had made during their 13-month stay in this place, the Japanese felt regret at leaving.

Chapter VIII

SITKA

In an instant it travels a thousand <u>ri</u>
What a grand spectacle
The paddlewheel steamship!

The two-masted ship on which the six Japanese sailed to Sitka, the easternmost Russian territory, was a solidly-built ship that had been made in America. Its expert craftsmanship surpassed any other ship in the harbor at Okhotsk.

The captain, the Japanese heard, had been born in Sitka. The oldest of 16 brothers, he traveled to St. Petersburg as a youth and studied ocean navigation. Even though it was the first voyage he had charted, he sailed into Okhotsk at the exact time he planned. The Japanese realized then that his skill was on a par with the American and English captains. Jirokichi was not sure of his rank, but his epaulettes were silver and many medals were affixed to his tunic.

English and American ships had more complicated surveying instruments than the Russians had. They would determine the positions of the heavenly bodies and then compute the ship's location down to the degree and seconds of latitude and longitude. In this respect, Jirokichi thought that the Russian navigation techniques were behind those of the other two countries. During storms there was much confusion on Russian ships, but the English and the Americans simply waited for conditions to calm down.

When Russian ship officers wanted to determine their position at sea [actually the speed] they threw a triangular-shaped board [log board] with a rope attached to it into the sea and it floated on the surface of the water. The rope was marked at intervals of six <u>shaku</u>. As the ship progressed, more rope was let out. An officer stood on deck holding an hour glass and counting the seconds.

Well, there were many cloudy or rainy days on the northern sea between Okhotsk and Alaska, but they were blessed with a favorable tailwind for most of the voyage. Thanks to this wind, they could reach Sitka in 50 days. It was then the beginning of August.[1]

Upon entering the bay, it was still one ri to the harbor. In back of the harbor, which faced southeast, was a mountain range about one ri high and covered with a thick growth of toga [hemlock]. The harbor entrance was five or six cho wide and in the center was an island that was nothing but solid rock. Twenty or thirty ships could be accommodated in the harbor at one time. The Japanese were surprised to see two big steamships docked there when they arrived.

Wind conditions were not favorable, so a bigger ship had to pull the ship from Okhotsk into the harbor. Because it had already become dark, the drifters were told to stay on board ship that night.

Sitka was located at about 57° N. latitude and 242° E. longitude according to Jirokichi. It was an island situated at the southernmost end of Russian territory in North America. The Russian-American Company branch office had been established there in recent years. Now it had become a flourishing trading post with ships from many countries coming and going through the harbor.[2]

Jirokichi was told that the governor of this post was a man born in Sweden (!) by the name of Adolf Karlovich Etolin. From being a ship captain he had received successive promotions until he received this position in the Russian government service. Etolin's wife was also Swedish-born.[3]

The governor lived in a castle on a fortress-like hill high above the town. It could be seen towering over the surrounding landscape far out to sea. The magnificent mansion was five stories tall and 50 or 60 ken square. The approach to the castle was by a long zig-zag flight of stairs with a railing. For defense, cannons were set up here and there and guards stood at attention. In front of the castle was a roofed gate. A large bell used to announce emergencies was

hanging inside the wall surrounding the residence. Since it
was lower than the wall, the bell could not be seen from the
harbor.[4]

Behind the castle was a church with a big clock set in
the steeple. To one side of the castle grounds and above the
wharf there were storehouses for cargo from the ships. The
shipyard was set back about a half cho from the coast. A big
bell near by was used as a signal for men to go to work. In
the southern part of the settlement there were three long
buildings which served as barracks for the soldiers.

Well, the governor gave orders for the Japanese to be
housed in a building two or three cho from his residence.
They all lived together in one room and were given adequate
food, clothing and tobacco. Even provided with a manservant,
they could pass each day in ease.

Living in the same building as the drifters were two
men said to be studying geography, particularly latitude and
longitude. There was also a sawyer, a controller, as well as
trader living there with their wives. They all shared a
kitchen about eight jo square. One room in the building was
shut off from the others and was used as the governor's
private sitting-room.

The Russians had come here about forty years before.
The Japanese observed that western nations spent much money
on colonization, even if the territory appeared to be useless at
first glance. They seemed to be looking for far-reaching
possibilities in the future. Such was the case in Sitka. The
Russians opened up this uncultivated land, colonized it, and
guided the barbaric natives with a benevolent heart
[according to Jirokichi]. It appeared that nations did this
with no immediate profit in mind. Because of their wealth,
they could afford to overlook setbacks while setting their
sights on the possibility of profits in years to come.

The Japanese soon realized that Sitka was completely
different from Kamchatka and Okhotsk in that cargo ships
from many countries gathered here and international trade
was actively pursued. The goods being bought and sold

seemed to be of higher quality than what they had seen in the other Russian settlements. Many Swedish traders came to Sitka. They did not have their own ships, but simply rented space and gave it up when they moved on.[?]

The climate in the area was relatively mild and there was little snow. The heaviest snowfall amounted to only seven or eight sun. The area was closed in by mountains to the north and was open to the sea in the south. Because of its proximity to the mountains this settlement received much rain. In a place called Adams [?] there were hot springs which were said to have a remarkable effect on all ailments.[5]

Cannons were set up in three locations in Sitka. Below the shipyards five cannons mounted on stands pointed in all four directions. Below the castle gate there were four or five gun carriages with cannons and five or six cannons on the ground. Also, along the stone embankment about 14 cannons were lined up among piles of projectiles.

In the mountains about one ri from the town there lived a tribe of Indians called Korushi [Kolosh].[6] There was said to be a population of 4000 in all. The Japanese were told that ever since the Russians had occupied the area the natives had shown much animosity toward them. In 1802 the Russian community was completely destroyed and many of the settlers were massacred. To quell the disturbances the Russians called for many fierce dogs to be brought out from their country. When the dogs were set upon the invaders their snarls kept the Indians at bay and the atrocities declined. Some Russians conjectured that the Indians were encouraged by the English who were establishing settlements further south. They were even said to have given guns to the natives. The Russians detested the tricky nature of the English.

The Kolosh were short---about five shaku tall and dark-skinned. Both men and women had long hair. The women wore it parted in the middle, pulled back and hanging down their backs. Their only clothing was a large square woolen cloth slung over one shoulder and tied there. Not all of the body was covered so one could see that they wore no loincloth or drawers. They always walked around carrying a wooden spear. The Japanese could not understand a word they said. They were always wary of the Indians because of the ferocious expressions on their faces.

Kolosh men and women had pierced noses and ears. Many rings were inserted with tassles attached. The men smeared something red on their faces---perhaps red ochre, berry juice or something obtained from tree roots. Bracelets were worn on both arms, and rings were on all five fingers of each hand.

The women also daubed their faces with red ochre and even rubbed it in their hair. Each woman's lower lip protruded over one sun. A ring made of horn was inserted in it and at night a wooden pin was put through the lip and nose ring locking her mouth shut. Thus a woman could not say a thing after going to bed. Men did not follow this custom.
Some 300 or so Kolosh had adopted the Russian way of life. They were employed by the Company during the day and returned to their homes at night. These people usually wore cast-off western clothing. The Indians who lived further back in the mountains were comparatively vicious and uncivilized.

Five or six cho into the mountains there was a sandy river spanned by a crude bridge. On the other side was a Kolosh settlement. The Japanese thought that their dwellings resembled the Ainu huts in Ezo. Some were put together with ropes.

Jirokichi frequently went to the Kolosh open market to look around. There were melons, as well as other kinds of fruit, wild birds, animals, fish and shellfish displayed. "Akko! Akko!," they called out. This meant "Please buy".

If the Kolosh women were given tobacco they showed much pleasure. Some of the Russian men used these women for their amusement. After taking liberties with them, there would be tell-tale smudges left on their bodies and other men would tease them about it.[7]

While the drifters were in Sitka the chief of the Kolosh died. They observed the cremation rites which took place out-of-doors. A great crowd of Indians came to view the body. Each person would sweep a branch over the body and cry out madly.

In November the Indians would wade into the cold river up to their necks. This was a kind of morning ablution. When the Russians rang a bell to announce nightfall, the Indians would jump out of the river and come running from all directions creating a great clamor. They could walk barefoot on the ice and snow. The Japanese were told that after they had soaked their bodies in the icy water they felt warm when they came out, so they could do that.

The Russian bath house was styled after the Turkish steam bath and was operated by the government. All people used the same place and there was no fee. It opened in the afternoon, first the men came, and in the evening the women could enter the bath house. In Kamchatka and Okhotsk there was just one government-operated bath house, too, but some families had their own bathrooms in their homes. In those places the men and women used the bath house on different days, but all were Turkish steam bath style. Throughout the year it was the custom to take a bath once every seven days.

The bathroom was about about three by five ken and six shaku high. It had glass windows. There were four platforms arranged like steps where the bathers could sit. At one end of the room there was a stone fireplace with an iron grill over the fire. Rocks and scrap iron were placed on the grill while the fire burned beneath. A copper pipe extended through the roof to let out the smoke. After the fire had burned vigorously for about three hours and the stones and scrap iron had become red hot, the smoke passage was blocked thus confining the heat. Water was carried in wooden buckets and poured over the rocks and iron two or three times to create steam. The entrance to the bathroom was kept closed for about two hours to keep in the steam. In the evening lamps were set up in the room.

There was a boiler in the bath house where a watchman was always in attendance. Each bather was first allowed three <u>sho</u> of water and later was given five <u>sho</u>, no more than that. The bathers soaped themselves all over so the dirt would come off easily. They later used cherry branches with the leaves still on them to beat their bodies. They would also rub themselves with a towel to make their bodies even hotter.

One time when the drifters were in Kamchatka, Rokubei and Jirokichi mistakenly entered the bath house on the day designated for women. The crowd of girls stared at the two men, bent their little finger in front of their thumb and laughed. The Japanese didn't understand what they meant by the gesture but later found out that they thought the Japanese male organ was small.

During the drifters' stay in Sitka a warning of a possible Indian raid was issued. Previous to that there had been an incident in which ten or twenty soldiers went into the mountains to get firewood. About a hundred Kolosh suddenly appeared in dugout canoes and began throwing spears. Since the soldiers were up against great odds, they ran away instead of attacking when the Kolosh stole all their saws and hatchets. The soldiers immediately reported the incident to the governor who had a steamship sail out to catch the thieves. Then there was a rumor that the Indians would attack the fort in revenge.

The Japanese were thrown into a panic by the fear of a battle and refused to go out. But the governor pooh-poohed the idea saying, "You mice! What are you afraid of? If they come they will all be killed."

Complete preparations had been made to meet any emergency. Cannons had been carried out of the armory, as well as many other weapons. The sight of all the armaments made the drifters all the more apprehensive.

The entrance to the river was blocked with a big steamship and another ship. Big boats were joined together with ropes at the bow and stern and firmly tied to rings attached to posts on both shores. Platforms were put on top of the boats and cannons were set on them. The gun barrels faced both ways. Two or three guards watched over each boat, and soldiers set up an encampment on the shore ready for combat. This strong defense system evidently frightened the Kolosh enough so they did not carry out the attack.

Sometime before this the Kolosh chief had been questioned as to the reason for the raid in the mountains. From his reply the Russians were quite sure that the English had incited the violence.

A grand banquet was held at the governor's castle once a month. Officers, accompanied by their wives and other relatives, attended. When the eating and drinking was at its height, husbands and wives joined hands and danced. The governor and his wife also danced to the lively music.

There was also an exhibition of dancing performed by young people at the party. They wore short-sleeved costumes made of sheer silk material. It was so thin that one could plainly see their skin underneath. They wore a silk scarf on their heads and waved a cloth as they danced.

In an adjoining room the stiff figure of the Kolosh chief could be seen. From this the Japanese conjectured that the governor arranged such parties not only because he liked drinking and dancing but also to curry favor with the Indians. It was one of his schemes for taming their ferocious nature.

One time when some Indians were raking the governor's yard, Etolin nodded to them and said to the Japanese, "In that way we will finally civilize them and they will act like human beings. Give us 14 or 15 more years and they will obey and follow our orders to work. Then maybe all of the Kolosh can come to my parties." The Japanese were very impressed with his idealistic thinking.

Southeast of the town there was a sandy beach. At the end was a big rock about five <u>ken</u> square that projected out into the sea. On top of it there was a bench where the governor sat and watched the fishermen catching the fish to serve to his guests.

The natives used a method to catch flounder that resembled seine fishing in Japan. When they had a big catch, a pulley was used to pull in the net. The Alaskan flounder was huge, sometimes as long as one jo. The skin was seven or eight bu thick and so oily it had to be thrown away. The edible flesh was over one shaku thick and tasted very good.

The cove was narrow where the fishing boats were anchored. The coastlands spread out for five or six cho along the shore and were thickly forested. There were footboards laid for a walking path. At the end of the woods there was a clear stream about three ken wide. Many salmon could be seen there. If one walked across a wooden bridge and turned left and walked several cho, one came to a pond about one cho wide and five or six cho long where the settlers enjoyed skating and other amusements.

Officials came from St. Petersburg to collect wild species of birds, animals and insects in this place. They showed the specimens to the Japanese and explained how they preserved the birds and soaked the snakes in alcohol. Insects were dried and suspended on wires and placed in a box. Pressed flowers were put between sheets of paper.

The Indians used the crossbow method for shooting wild geese. They would lie face down and pull the bow with their legs. The arrows were inserted in a kind of tube. In June when the wild geese were molting and during the breeding season the geese could be caught with one's bare hands as they couldn't fly well.

The Russians' houses and the barracks were built with big logs. The soldiers' barracks were two-story buildings about 30 ken long and six or seven ken wide. The foundation was made of logs nearly three shaku in diameter. In the center of the barracks was a hallway with staircases at both ends and in the center. About half of the soldiers had their families with them.

For the soldiers with families each was given a space about two ken long and nine shaku wide marked off with wooden partitions. Below these walls there was a six or seven sun wide indentation in the floor full of packed sand. This was to stop the spread of fire. For lighting there was a big glass window, and beside that was a chimney. Each soldier was supplied with an iron stove and an iron pot so his wife could cook for them. To separate the cooking spaces a piece of white canvas was hung. The living spaces were small but they were kept neat and clean.

There ware many paddlewheel ships in Sitka harbor when the drifters were there. These ships were called "steamboats," they said.[8] Some were bigger than others. The large ones had a more complex mechanism than the smaller ones. The small ones were only three or four shaku square and not over a shaku high. A wooden cover was kept over it so the inner mechanism could not be seen. Only one person was needed to operate it. He fueled it, operated the rudder and he had a way to send emergency messages to other ships. The mechanism was precise but not complex.

The big steamships had paddlewheels on each side. They were about twice as high as the gunwales. The wheels had covers over them with crosspieces nailed on them. These crosspieces were used like a staircase. These ships had no mast. [This is an error.] The hulls were shaped like a pharmacist's medicine mortar [rounded and oblong]. As a rule the ship could travel 400 Russian miles in a day and a night, as they did not have to be concerned with adverse winds or darkness.

On the big ships two copper boilers were installed at mid-ship. A wooden barrier was constructed around them to prevent people from getting too close to the hot metal. One big pot was set inside an even larger pot. Fire burned in the smaller one and water filled the space between them. At the ship's stern there was a device that pumped sea water into the boilers constantly, so there was no need to worry about the water drying up. Around the top of the boilers there were small holes stopped up with plugs. Through these holes the temperature and the amount of water could be gauged. When the sea water boiled, salt gushed out of the holes.

Two copper pipes resembling masts extended from atop the boilers. The one on the outside pot was about 9/10 shorter than the one on the inside pot. There was also a big copper pipe coming out of the side of the boiler nearest the stern. That pipe divided in two and these pipes extended up toward the prow. (Jirokichi did not understand the purpose of these.)

When the inside pot became full of ashes the force of the steam spewed them out. Ashes flew every which way with great force.

On top of each boiler in the center were two tubes with pistons inside. These pistons were attached to a horizontal bar. When the water in the boiler reached the boiling point the steam holes were opened and power gushed out making the pistons go up and down, and this in turn moved the horizontal bar which turned the cogwheel. As the cogwheel revolved, the shaft moved, and this made the wheels rotate and paddle water. Then the ship moved smoothly over the water.

Two people took hold of the iron handles that regulated the opening and closing of the valves where the steam gushed out. The boilerman always stood in front of the boilers keeping an eye on them.

To stop the ship steam was released from an opening on the side, and subsequently the wheels stopped rotating. To make the ship move in reverse they simply opened different valves and the ship went backwards. Steam was also used to regulate the movement of the rudder, so the ship could be steered in different directions.

The metal on the ship was polished by hand every day. The pistons fairly sparkled in the sunlight.

One day Governor Etolin invited Jirokichi to ride to a nearby island on one of the steamships. He said, "Look at the mechanism carefully, Jirokichi, and when you return home perhaps you can build the same kind of ship." He added, "Since these ships have been plying the China route they have been attracting a lot of attention and throngs of sightseers come out to see them."

Jirokichi tried to analyze and remember the complicated mechanism but sometimes it boggled his mind and made his head spin. He was sorry after he returned home that he had not paid better attention.

Jirokichi described the ship that he rode on as being about 30 ken long and 10 ken wide. It was furnished with 30 cannons.[9] Over 100 koku of coal was stored in the hold of the ship, but that day they were burning wood. Using coal was said to be more advantageous on long voyages because more could be stored in a small space.

On the island Jirokichi noticed that water power was being used to saw wood. He was told that previously many saws were needed but now just one could do the job. The water-powered saw moved smoothly and well.

Jirokichi was asked one day about the drifters from Echigo who had come to Sitka a few years before. [See Introduction, Note #10.] He was told, "The drifters that came before you were obstinate people and we couldn't understand their character. They hid in boxes the nice clothes and caps that we gave to them and instead of wearing them they walked around in kimonoes and geta [wooden clogs]. The townspeople laughed at them." Then he said to Jirokichi, "On the contrary you people have a neat appearance and are wonderful guests."

One day the Japanese were told that the governor had made plans for them to be taken back to Japan. He had received an order from Irkutsk saying, "The drifters are to be repatriated to Japan." It was explained to them that it would be dangerous to go near the Japanese coast so they would be taken as far as one of the Kurile Islands [north of Ezo] and they would have to make their way from there in a baidarka. It was suggested that they practice maneuvering the Russian boat made of leather and wood.

The baidarkas were about three <u>ken</u> long, three <u>shaku</u> wide and two <u>shaku</u> deep. The boat narrowed on both ends. They had a wooden frame, and seal skins which had been sewn together were stretched over about half of the boat. There were three holes for people to sit. They fit so snugly in the holes that no water could get in when they were paddling the boat. Even if the waves were high, there was no danger of getting wet. The paddlers sat in the boat with their legs stretched out in front of them. The paddle was wide and about four <u>shaku</u> long and flat on both ends. The boat cut through the water smoothly and quickly.

The baidarka had the added quality of being collapsible. It could be folded up and one person could carry four or five of them on his back when he climbed mountains or forded streams.

Two or three days before the Japanese left Sitka the governor instructed their servant to bring them to his residence. Near the rear entrance of his mansion there were chimes hanging from the ceiling. If one pulled the copper wire attached to them, they chimed like wind bells. A servant then appeared to guide the guests, for their manservant was not allowed to proceed any further. The drifters were taken to a drawing room on the fourth [second?] floor. The floor of the room looked like painted stone pavement. The six Japanese lined up to await the governor's appearance. When he entered he informed them, "In just two more days arrangements will have been completed to repatriate you to your homeland. We have received orders from the capital to take you as far as Etorofu, but since this island has inconvenient access to Matsumae we intend to take you to Atsukeshi [on the east coast of Hokkaido]. I wanted you to know that."

Then the governor's wife set six glasses before the Japanese and poured the liquor herself. No servants were in the room, only the governor and his wife and the drifters. Parting greetings were regretfully exchanged, for they knew they would probably never meet again.

On the wall in the parlor was a splendid wall clock. The governor could not help but notice that the drifters took much interest in it and said, "Oh, that's perfect! You must take a souvenir back to your homeland. This was also mentioned in the letter I received from the capital. I will present that clock to you." The governor stood up and removed it from the wall himself and handed it over to the Japanese. They were overwhelmed by his generosity and insisted that they could not accept such a wonderful gift, but the governor added, "In Russia it is considered a discourtesy to turn down a gift. It is especially true in such a case for this is not a gift from myself but a highly honorable token of friendship from our government."[10]

The governor then opened a door and beckoned to the Japanese to come into another room. There he pointed to a portrait of the Russian emperor hanging on the wall and said, "This is our present emperor, His Majesty Nikolai Pavlovich [Nicholas I]. The Japanese courteously faced the portrait and bowed. "Well, now please take this clock home," the governor said, "and present it to the chief magistrate in your country."

"In Japan," the drifters explained, "the Emperor resides in Kyoto. The next in rank is in Edo [the Shogun], and there are other magistrates in each province."

"You come from various provinces, so the governors are different, aren't they?"

The Japanese smiled and said that they all hailed from the same province.

"Well, in that case, please present the clock to the governor of your province," he begged.

The governor's wife also presented the drifters with ten charcoal drawings of houses and churches. They had been brought from St. Petersburg.

The sailors were apprehensive about how to handle the precious clock so the governor said that he would speak to the ship's captain about it. They left it in his cabin and it remained in his custody all during the subsequent voyage.

Chapter IX

TO ETOROFU

The boom of the cannons
Fog breaks up to reveal the mountains of Ezo.

Finally the sailing date was set for the middle of March [1843]. The ship was the <u>Promysel</u> commanded by Captain Aleksander Nikolai Gavrilov, aged 24 or 25.[1] There were about 30 crew members, including two doctors. Two or three sailors were accompanied by their wives and children.

When the ship left Sitka harbor many men and women came to see them off shouting, "Ha-ro, Ha-ro" [Ura! Ura! - Hurrah!]. The captain stayed up on a high place on the ship to acknowledge their send-off greetings for a long time.

The sea was sometimes stormy and rough, in fact, the Japanese sailors thought conditions were just as bad as what they had encountered off Toni when they met with the shipwreck on the <u>Chojamaru</u>. Sometimes the waves swept over the entire ship, but much to their surprise, the Russian ship, due to its superior construction, could withstand the force of the waves and consequently suffered no damage.

The drifters could not understand the reason for it, but the doctors insisted on examining them every day. The examinations included taking blood samples. Jirokichi said to the doctor one day, "As you can see, I am healthy, so I don't need these consultations." The doctor replied, "No, we receive pay from the Emperor to do this, so we must not be negligent in carrying out our duties. We are accompanying you on this voyage for this purpose, so please be patient." Jirokichi was deeply impressed by their concern and he never refused the examination again.

One time a Russian sailor accidently fell from the top of the mast and broke his leg. It was a very serious injury and they said it would be difficult for him to make a complete recovery, so the captain gave orders for the doctors to amputate his leg.

The surgeon tied down the patient at the thigh and knees with strong cord, and with a surgical knife he scooped out the infected part. He cut through the muscle completely at the joint and the injured leg fell to the floor. The wound was covered with ointment and bandaged. After it healed it was covered with a pad stuffed with cotton, and a wooden leg was attached. The sailor could walk freely and it didn't seem any different from a real leg.

When Jirokichi reflected on the character of the various peoples he met, he thought that the Americans from the northern part of the country had a better character than those from the south. Nantucket people were especially refined like high-class people in Japan. The [American] women were all beautiful.

When Jirokichi thought about the people he ordinarily associated with, he said that the Americans and the English were calm and soft-spoken. They were also intelligent and sharp. [He used the word kibin, meaning shrewd, sharp, alert.] When he compared them with the Russians he thought the latter were even more gentle to the extent of being somewhat dull. He added that Russians had excellent memories. If they heard even a trifling thing once, they would remember it. He also said, "There were Englishman who were ingenious at contriving schemes, but everywhere Americans had likeable dispositions.[2] "If our country would trade with America," he said, "we would not come to any harm." He added, "All the countries' circumstances are good at this time, if they wish to send big ships to our country for trade we should admit those from America, England and Russia, not any others."

Jirokichi noted that the English language was used in many countries. No matter where he traveled, they used English. He thought it was just like the use of Edo-ben [Edo dialect] in Japan.

When men joined together to lift some heavy object they shouted in unison like they do in Japan. Also when they shouted assent, "Shochi, shochi! [O.K.!] in many countries they all shout "Hey!" or "Hi!".

One day the Russian captain said to Jirokichi, "If Japan calls out its army and tries to capture us, we intend to let down a boat and land immediately and a battle will break out. The Emperor gave me orders, 'If Japan shows a rude attitude, comply with their orders, land, and submit to being tied up with a rope. If your ship is late in coming back, a big army will be dispatched to back you up.'"

Just before setting sail Jirokichi heard a lower rank officer say, "This time, of course the Japanese will not fire on us." Jirokichi doubted his words but upon approaching Ezo, sure enough he was right. This was because of the relaxation made in the edicts regarding firing on foreign ships approaching the shores of Japan.[3]

Jirokichi noted that there was little harmony in the diplomatic relations between the Dutch and the Russians. This was because Russia frequently requested help from the Dutch in seeking trade negotiations with the Japanese. The evasive answers they received from the Dutch angered the Russians.[4]

If American ships came near Dutch territory they were fired upon and driven away, so in retaliation for that, the Americans did the same when Dutch ships came near their shores. It was said that the English advised the Dutch to do this. This shows that the Dutch and the English wanted to monopolize the trade for themselves.

In Russia they said, "New Dutch." It meant "New Hollander" and at this time it was another name for Australia (actually Java). Dutch merchant ships came and went from there frequently, the drifters ware told by Englishmen. Jirokichi was shown a map of this territory and the trade routes were pointed out.

Jirokichi also heard that Russia was using many Aleut people to settle the islands in the proximity of Ezo. When the Promysel was about 200 ri from Ezo he could see the Futago

[twin] Islands in the direction of east by southeast. He reported, "If our country doesn't do something with them soon, Westerners will take possession of them. It would be regrettable."

After sailing for about two months the captain of the Promysel informed the Japanese, "In two or three days we will be able to see Japanese mountains." On a world map they had drawn a line to show their voyage. "This is the course we are taking," he said as he showed them the map. Just as he said, the mountains of Ezo appeared on the horizon in a day or two. With a certain navigation device they could even gauge the height of the mountains.

"If the Japanese don't attack us, we would like to pick up a small rock on the seacoast as proof that we returned the drifters," the Russians said. Instead of a rock, they picked up a willow tree five or six shaku long, roots and all, that floated by. The captain was very pleased with this Japanese willow and said he would keep it carefully. In Sanoitsu [?] there weren't any trees like it, but there were many willow trees in Russia.

At a point about 30 ri from Etorofu Island the Russians test fired their cannons. While doing this the tow rope snapped and the cannon mount was damaged. Then they had to take time out to repair it, for they said, "If we are fired upon by the Japanese, we must be able to return shots. Our equipment must be in good condition."

For that test, iron projectiles weighing over one kamme 500 momme packed with one sho of gunpowder were fired. Along with some of the Russian sailors, Jirokichi climbed up the mast to see that sight. The ball flew over the surface of the rough sea appearing and then disappearing at intervals as it pierced the high waves. They followed the course of the projectile until it was out of sight. The Russians very carefully determined its range saying it reached a point two Russian miles away. They thought this was not powerful enough to use for warfare, so for the second test they used a lead projectile. This time it flew over five miles. Lead was heavier than iron so it flew with greater force and a farther distance.

As the Russian ship approached Etorofu the fog was so thick that visibility was nil. The captain ordered the cannons fired. After discharging 14 or 15 shots the fog completely disappeared and the mountains on the island clearly appeared before their eyes. They searched carefully but they could not find any fortifications on that coast. The ship proceeded along the shore between Etorofu and Kunashiri. The wind had died down and the tide fluctuated rapidly there, so there was a constant danger of hitting a shoal. The sailors raised their voices in a ballad chorus and held up an oar as if it were a sword indicating certain death. Some shouted, "Stick to it!" or "I don't want to become bait for the fish." Some were more resigned to the danger and said, "If we drown now, it is our destiny."

The captain stood at the gunwale giving commands with a worried expression on his face. Everybody cooperated and they finally escaped the danger.

A boat was let down with some sailors in it to go and get fresh water on the island. A long time elapsed and they still didn't come back. One of the officers said to Jirokichi, "I wonder if they have been killed by the Japanese. I'm sorry, but you must go and search for them." Just as he was about to disembark the boat came back safely.

Originally by the order of the Russian government the Japanese were to be taken back to Etorofu, but the governor in Sitka advised Captain Gavrilov to take them to Atsukeshi. The captain decided to give this a try and on May 21st at about 2 p.m. they came near Oguro Island in the Atsukeshi offing. It was only about six or seven cho in circumference.

When they had come within about two cho of the coast the captain said, "I think there are human habitations in this vicinity." He repeatedly searched with his binoculars but he could not confirm it. Just then a south wind came up which carried the ship around to the other side of the island near Atsukeshi. A baidarka was let down and a sailor got in it to have a look around. He was given orders to go only up to the shoreline. Soon he returned and reported that no houses were in sight. The captain said to the Japanese, "Since we cannot find any sign of inhabitants here, I don't think we should let you disembark."

(Later the drifters found out that the houses in Atsukeshi were hidden behind Oguro Island so they could not be seen from the shore. Rokubei had come to Kushiro, which is only about 10 ri from Atsukeshi, in his youth. The other drifters had been to Shamen, which is seven or eight ri from Kushiro, but they didn't know the name "Atsukeshi". They had even been under the impression that some parts of Ezo were Russian territory. They were surprised that the Russians knew details about the shoreline.)

Well, Captain Gavrilov continued to peer through his binoculars and finally he sighted one house near the shore and a man on horseback. Rokubei looked too and declared, "In that case, we would like to go ashore." The captain assented saying, "If you wish, please do."

As soon as the Ezo mountains came into view, the Japanese had prepared for landing. They shaved the front of their heads and, having no pomade, they smoothed down the rest of their hair with water. Since they didn't have the traditional paper cord, they had to tie the topknot with hemp twine. They had also taken out the Chojamaru flag and changed into their ragged kimonos that they had worn while drifting. The Russians laughed, but they explained that they didn't want to be mistaken for foreigners.

After exchanging parting words with the Russian captain and crew, the six Japanese got in bidarkas with all of their belongings. They had practiced maneuvering the boats in Sitka so they had no trouble making their way toward the house on the shore. Much to their disappointment, however it was not a human dwelling but just a crude shed. They knew they could not stay there so they talked over what to do next.

When they looked out over the water they spotted a Japanese ship. As it came nearer they could see that it was a sengokubune (1000-koku ship] of the Matsumae clan sailing toward Etorofu. "I know," one of them said, "we will ask them to take us aboard." They began paddling as hard as they could at the risk of life or death while waving the Chojamaru flag. But being favored with a tail wind, the big ship sailed so fast it was impossible to catch up with it.

Meanwhile, the Russians were repeatedly beckoning to the drifters to come back, so they turned and paddled toward the Promysel. Captain Gavrilov shouted, "That ship can take you home. Hurry! Get back on board our ship and we will overtake them." But as the Russian ship sped toward it, the Japanese ship sailed away faster and faster thanks to the tail wind. The Russian captain grimaced with disappointment.[5]

Since they found no evidence of human habitations around Atsukeshi, they decided to sail toward Etorofu. After sailing between Erori, a small island near the tip of Nemuro peninsula, and other islands in the vicinity, a strong wind came up blowing rain against the ship with great force. All they could do was sail with extreme caution among the islands around Etorofu and Kunashiri. When the seas calmed down a weight was lowered to determine the depth of the sea in this area. Because of the great navigational hazards the lamps on the ship were kept burning day and night. The captain and crew never so much as took a nap during this time.

On the morning of May 23rd the wind changed to the south and the weather cleared up. The ship passed between Etorofu and Kunashiri and into the western offing of Etorofu. When they were about 3 1/2 ri into the Furubetsu offing the captain ordered two boats let down. Six Russian sailors and Jirokichi were told to take a gun and ten buckets to get water. "In that mountain gorge over there, there surely must be fresh water," the captain said. Jirokichi thought it was doubtful but the captain insisted they try. "If only Russian people land, there is a chance they will be captured. Please go with them as an interpreter," he asked Jirokichi.

Well, they went on shore and looked around. There was a river near a hamlet called Oito, so they took water from there and returned to the ship. Just then they spotted an

Ainu boat making for Oito, but as soon as the people in the boat realized they were foreigners they fled.

Finally when the Promysel came to within about two ri of the Furubetsu coast they could see the masts of six or seven Japanese ships docked in the harbor. There seemed to be fairly many houses in the town, so everyone agreed that this would be a good place to land.

At about 2 p.m. when they were only about one ri from the coast an Ainu boat came near the Promysel to size up the foreign ship. A Japanese man in the boat hid under a rush mat and pretended to be sleeping. As soon as the drifters realized there was a Japanese person on board they couldn't help but cry out. Startled at the sound of their voices, the man under the mat sat up and yelled, "Who on earth are you?" They answered, "We are Ecchu people. Six years ago we were shipwrecked off the coast of Toni in Oshu and drifted on the open sea. Now we are being brought back by the Russians."

There were seven men in the boat, including three Ainu people and this man who turned out to be a subordinate samurai of the Matsumae clan named Kobayashi Chogoro. He came out to examine the foreign ship, not in any official capacity, but out of personal curiosity. He had covered himself with the mat because he was shrinking in fear at seeing the foreigners.

After the Russians beckoned to them, the men in the boat climbed up the rope ladder onto the big ship. Captain Gavrilov invited Kobayashi into his cabin, and food and drinks were served. Besides eating and drinking, Jirokichi said, this brutish fellow talked loudly and even had the nerve to initiate the exchange of sword tassles with the Russian captain. As the liquor soon made Kobayashi drunk he began drinking toasts and kissing in the Russian tradition. The three Ainu, as well as three other Japanese named Shinzo, Matabei and Sankichi, were similarly treated on the deck. They were so pleased they began dancing. The drifters felt that the Russians were treating everyone as a parting token for them.

Just when the mood was happy on both sides an unfortunate incident occurred. Kobayashi, now obviously intoxicated, suddenly unsheathed his sword and thrust it toward the captain. By showing him the keenness of the Japanese sword, it was his intention to warn the foreigners of Japan's military prowess. The Russian captain's facial expression immediately changed to chagrin, and he automatically reached for his sword. While showing Kobayashi how the Russian sword could be bent and straightened out again, he muttered, "Your swords may be hard, but they don't bend. We can bend ours freely, and with one swoop behead ten people with only the tip of the blade. Moreover, I also have a pistol and a musket." The provoked captain looked at Kobayashi and added, "Your sword will be of no use whatever if I use these," as he pointed to his guns.

Of course this was said in Russian and Kobayashi could not understand. Jirokichi stood between them and at various times tried to interpret and mediate. He tried to placate the captain by saying, "This man only wants to show you his wonderful sword. He is feeling in a happy mood and does not intend any ill will."

Finally they put away their swords and the incident was settled peacefully. Then Captain Gavrilov requested a written statement saying that Kobayashi took delivery of six Japanese drifters. Kobayashi bade Shinzo to fetch his inkstone and brush from the boat so that he could write the receipt. On the paper he also wrote a poem by Kakinomoto Hitomaro:

Faintly the bay appears
In the mist of dawn.

The paper was then handed over to the Russian captain.

Captain Gavrilov than handed him some thirty sheets of paper with European-style writing on them. Kobayashi proceeded to loosen the knot on the strap of the sheath of his sword and suggested they trade straps. Upon interpreting this gesture, the Russian captain agreed.

At that point Jirokichi said to Kobayashi, "You know it will take at least a month for this ship to return, so I am afraid that they will suffer from a shortage of drinking water. We were not really asked by the ship's officers to do this, but since they took care of us for a long time, I beg of you to manage this for us."

Kobayashi answered, "If we give water to them, the ship will have to go to Hakodate and there they would be subjected to questioning by shogunate officials. I am sure they would be beaten off by cannon fire before they reached shore, however. Fortifications are set up all along the coast and they are prepared to shoot at any time. I, myself, could give orders not to shoot immediately, but I think it would be better in this situation for the ship to go back right away. He then warned Jirokichi, "You will be taken to Edo. Now if you are not ordered to leave your homeland, never forget my favor to you. I will spare you an investigation at this time. Please report this to your interrogators."

Kobayashi's answer to Jirokichi's request was in this vein. But again the drifters begged him to supply the Russians with water. The Russian captain asked, "What did he say?" The drifters replied rather evasively, "Kobayashi can stop the bombardment from the coast."

The captain explained, "We have brought back Japan's children. If one sees home someone's lost child, they expect to be treated by the parents." He then asked Jirokichi, "What rank is this fellow anyway?"

"He seems to be just an underling," Jirokichi replied. "He does, doesn't he?", the captain said with a smile.

At that time Kobayashi was wearing old work pants and a _haori_ and looked rather shabby.

Kobayashi took the papers, the sword strap, and he even picked up a cigar butt when he left. He then got in his boat to return to Furubetsu. The drifters shook hands with Captain Gavrilov, and he kissed each of them. Then the six Japanese got into two boats, Tasaburo, Rokubei and

Shichizaemon got in one and Hachizaemon, Kinzo and Jirokichi got in the other, carefully carrying the precious clock they had received in Sitka. As their boats separated from the big ship they shouted farewells. The captain and all the crew stood on the deck watching through their binoculars. The Russians hoisted a white flag showing that negotiations had gone smoothly.[6]

It was evening when the drifters stepped on land at Furubetsu on Etorofu Island. Kobayashi had arrived before them. Ten samurai of the Matsumae clan, with guns slung over their shoulders, were there to meet the returnees. Also many sightseers had gathered. The next morning the white sails of the Promysel could be seen about seven or eight ri out to sea.

Chapter X

THE RETURN HOME

Fires along the coast
Not to help strangers
But alas! To keep them away from our country.

After the friendly Russian people on the ship gave endless farewells to the drifters, the six returnees landed at the harbor of Furubetsu on Etorofu island, Japanese territory. At this place ships gathered from all over Japan. The drifters were elated to meet sailors from their home province.

Upon arriving at the official headquarters on the island the men were given underwear. It had become second nature for them to wear Western-style clothing, but now they felt they were really back in Japan. A full 4 years had passed since they last stepped on Japanese soil.

After Etorofu, the nostalgic path home was long and difficult. After a careful investigation at Furubetsu the men were taken to Matsumae. There they were questioned extensively by clan officials. From there they were sent to Edo accompanied by clan officials arriving on the 14th day of the intercalary 9th month.

In Edo the Toyama sailors were put in the custody of Oguroya Choemon at his inn at Koishikawa's Kasugacho. The interrogation by shogunate officials was to be strict and lengthy. Perhaps their minds were relaxed at last, but during the first month of their stay in Edo, Shichizaemon passed away.

The repatriates were kept in detention in Edo for three years. At last in December, 1846, they were permitted to make a temporary visit to their hometowns. But in May of the following year they were again summoned to Edo. The examination this time dragged on for over a year. It may be more appropriate to call it a kind of internment. [Editor's words.]

During the second examination in Edo Hachizaemon took sick and died, so he was not destined to enjoy living with his family again.

It was during the second interrogation period that Koga Kinichiro listened to Jirokichi's narrative for the eventual Bandan literary work. Koga states in the preface of his book that he met with Jirokichi only five or six times, but in truth he must have talked with him more times in private. It would not have been safe to reveal this fact for it was prohibited for returned drifters to disseminate any information about foreign places unless it was officially sanctioned by the shogunate.

The government did not approve of such a practice [relating overseas experiences on an unofficial basis] but this was a special case where protocol was overlooked because of the importance of the information at this time.

Other scholars sat in on the discussions between Koga and Jirokichi. As they listened to the detailed descriptions and valuable pieces of information their knowledge of foreign places increased rapidly. The scholars were so impressed they were inspired to write poems about the exotic places and events as Jirokichi described them. These private meetings were interrupted many times because of the interrogation procedures of the Bakufu [government] officials.

The great amount of material gleaned from the Koga-Jirokichi talks was researched, revised and arranged, and along with the extensive number of illustrations drawn by the narrator, it materialized into Bandan [Stories of Barbaric Places].

The three-volume work was hand copied several times, but like other sea-drifting records it was kept out of the sight of the general public. Only selected scholars with a special interest in foreign affairs were allowed to peruse the work.

At this time Toyama was part of the Kaga [now Kanazawa prefecture] Clan. This was said to be the wealthiest clan in Japan. The clock which was given to the drifters in Sitka was presented to Daimyo Maeda Nariyasu. This type of wind-up clock could be made in Japan at this time but such a timepiece was exceedingly rare. Also considering the fact that it had come from across the sea made it a great curiosity. Maeda wanted a complete record made of the story behind the clock. Endo Takenori, a famous mathematician, was asked to write it from listening to the drifters' talk. This came to be called Tokei Monogatari [The Story of the Clock]. Of the two books written about the Chojamaru event this was the glamorous one. Bandan was destined to be "the younger sister." The 24-volume Tokei Monogatari is abundantly sprinkled with colored pictures. It is indeed the most splendid of drifting records. [Strangely enough, as of this writing, this remarkable work has yet to be transcribed into modern Japanese.]

Bandan was copied more than Tokei Monogatari because it was considered more important. Even though it was kept out of the reach of the common people, we can say that it influenced Japanese history in a way, as it was read by government officials. Contrary to the narrowmindedness of the shogunate, it presented a wide view of the world.

A 24-volume set of Tokei Monogatari is in the possession of the Sonkei Kaku [Library] a private establishment endowed by the Maeda family foundation in Tokyo.

Among copies of Bandan that remain today, besides the three-volume set at the Bishop Museum in Honolulu, there is a two-volume set at the Toyo Bunka Library in Tokyo and a three-volume edition at the Kyoto University Library.

Well, after the second examination in Edo was over only four survivors of the Chojamaru disaster remained--- Tasaburo, Jirokichi, Kinzo and Rokubei. Then Tasaburo followed his shipmates to the grave only six months after returning home.

Little is known about the lives of the three survivors after settling down in their home towns. Kinzo was said to have become a salt merchant.

Jirokichi, who was 26 years old at the time of the shipwreck, was a so-called aimawashi-rank sailor handling various duties on board ship. [Aimawashi may be loosely translated as "handyman".] He was said to have the strength of a giant, which was borne out in some of his experiences overseas. He was also intelligent and had a keen memory. Moreover, he was endowed with an artistic sense. Among the drifters, he was certainly the most outstanding man.

When Jirokichi returned to his hometown to live, it had been eight years since he had left on the Chojamaru. Having been divorced previous to sailing, he had no home or family, so he was taken in by the family of his elder brother, Shichiroemon, who was already living in impoverished circumstances. An eye affliction hampered his opportunities to find gainful employment.

When Jirokichi was called to Edo in 1847 he and his brother were at a loss as to how to secure sufficient funds to make the trip. After explaining his great distress to the village elders, Shichiroemon succeeded in borrowing the necessary money to send his brother to Edo for more questioning.

Professor Takase Shigeo of Toyama University has done extensive research on this story and wrote Chojamaru no Hyoryu [The Drifting of the Chojamaru]. To his regret he has been unable to find out where Jirokichi died or where he is buried. His memory will live on, however, through the pages of Bandan.

NOTES AND REFERENCES

Introduction

1. During the seclusion period in Japan only the Dutch and the Chinese were allowed to carry on a tenuous trade comprising one ship a year through the port of Nagasaki. These foreign traders were isolated on a tiny fan-shaped island called Dejima within the city of Nagasaki.

2. Among all the drifting stories I have read involving rescues of Japanese seamen by whalers I have rarely come across any rescuers who were other than American, although the Russians offered shelter to drifters who were washed ashore. The Russians assisted in bringing them home. In the case of the drifters rescued by the Manhattan in 1845, the Japanese sailors were asked on their return what the nationality of their rescuers was. According to Sakamaki Shunzo in Japan and the United States 1790-1853, p. 22, the record states: "The nationality of the ship was unknown, but the waifs had agreed among themselves that it could not be either English or Russian, for according to hearsay such ships never saved people at sea."

3. The longest drifting odyssey on record for a Japanese is that of the Tokujomaru, Captain Jukichi. After drifting for 18 months without seeing any land, the three survivors were rescued off the coast of California on March 14, 1815.

   In 1832-33 the Hojunmaru drifted for 14 months on the Kuroshio current and three survivors were washed ashore in the vicinity of Cape Flattery (now Washington state). For more details on both events see The Shogun's Reluctant Ambassadors by the author.

4. All negotiations with foreign ships were carried out at the port of Nagasaki because it was the only place where there were interpreters.

5. The Kurile Islands extend from Kamchatka peninsula to the vicinity of Nemuro on the east coast of Hokkaido (formerly Ezo). At the time of the Chojamaru event Kunashiri, Etorofu, Shikotan and the Habomai Islands were Japanese. Under the Yalta agreement after World War II, the Soviet Union gained possession of these islands. Japan, however, still considers them their "Northern Territories" and has refused to agree to a peace treaty with the Soviet Union pending the return of what they consider their rightful territory.

6. Kodaiyu, a brilliant and resilient sea captain, who drifted to Russia in 1782 and was befriended by Catherine the Great at the capital, returned home in 1792. He was confined in Edo for the rest of his life. See The Shogun's Reluctant Ambassadors, Chap. VII.

7. From the introduction of Bandan by the editors, Yamori Kazuhiko and Murogo Nobuo, p. 26.

8. Several hand-copied editions of Bandan exist to this day. One three-volume set is in the possession of the Bishop Museum in Honolulu. This was procured by an American resident in Tokyo around 1912 when he was collecting material related to Commodore Perry's visit to Japan. George R. Carter, one-time governor of Hawaii, then acquired the book and later his son presented it to the museum. The book is inscribed:

    Gift of G. Robert Carter
    in memory of his father
    Gov. George R. Carter

    An interesting coincidence is that Gov. Carter was the grandson of Captain J. O. Carter who commanded the Harlequin on which the Chojamaru drifters sailed to Kamchatka. On the other side of the family, he was the grandson of Dr. Judd, with whom Jirokichi stayed in Honolulu.

9. From the editors' introduction to Bandan, pp. 7 and 30.

10. Tsudaiyu drifted to the Aleutians on the Wakamiyamaru where the survivors were rescued by the Russians. He got on board the Nadezhda, commanded by Admiral Krusenstern, when it made the first voyage around the world for the Russians. Their last stop before Kamchatka was at the Sandwich Islands in 1804. They hoped to buy pigs there, but were unsuccessful in making a deal with the natives. Tsudaiyu was finally brought back to Nagasaki in the same ship.

Zenmatsu was on the Inawakamaru when it was wrecked in 1805. After drifting for about 70 days they were rescued by the Tabour commanded by Capt. Cornelius Sole of Providence, Rhode Island. He took the Japanese to Honolulu. Zenmatsu arrived back in Nagasaki in 1807, the only member of the crew to survive. For more details see the Papers of the Hawaiian Historical Society, No. 18, October, 1931, the article by Y. Soga entitled "A Japanese Account of the First Recorded Visit of Shipwrecked Japanese to Hawaii". It is also mentioned in Amasa Delano's Narratives of Voyages and Travels, Boston, 1817.

The Echigo ship washed ashore at Wailuku in December, 1832 after having drifted 10 or 11 months. The four survivors stayed in Honolulu for about 11 months. With the help of Mr. W. French, a businessman in Honolulu, they were sent to Kamchatka and Sitka and eventually could get back to Japan. For details see The Hawaiian Spectator, Vol. 1, No. 3, July 1938.

NOTES

Chapter 1

1. A koku was a bale of rice equivalent to approximately 5 bushels or 180 liters. This measurement was used to describe the capacity of Japanese cargo ships.

Japanese-style dates are given with the era name first. Era names usually coincide with the reigns of Emperors but it is often arbitrary. The lunar calendar, in which all of the months (or "moons") were the same length, and an intercalary "leap month" was added about every three years, was used by the Japanese until 1873, when the Gregorian calendar was adopted. The lunar calendar was irregular in several respects making it difficult to calculate the exact equivalent with Western-style dates.

2.   Common people in the Edo period had but one name. Captain Heishiro sometimes went by the name of Yoshiokaya Heishiro. The captain had once been a patent medicine dealer. Yoshiokaya may have been the name of his former employer.

It was not unusual at this time for people, especially sailors, to change their names. This was sometimes done at the time of a crisis while hoping it would change their luck.

3.   The reader will notice that many calculations in this narrative are not stated exactly. The writer or narrator probably did this to avoid the embarrassment of possibly making a mistake.

4.   Japanese sailors of this period were very superstitious. They carried many talismans and ship charms, and often resorted to exorcism and divination when facing danger.

5.   The survivors of the Chojamaru incident heard after returning home that seven ships were lost in this storm.

6.   After returning home Tasaburo presented this scroll to the shogunate in Edo. It was later returned to Toyama and kept in Hachizaemon's home.

7.   Kompira is the guardian diety of seafarers according to Buddhist belief. Cutting their hair in the time of crisis was an act of purification before worshiping.

NOTES

Chapter II

1.   According to the log of the <u>James Loper</u>, the date of
        rescue was June 6 by Western reckoning. As for the
        location, Captain Cathcart determined it to be 30°43"
        latitude and 189°54" longitude.

2.   Later on when the drifters were in the Sandwich
        Islands, Rev. Dwight Baldwin mentioned what was
        undoubtedly this ship in an article he wrote about the
        <u>Chojamaru</u> men. He said that it was the <u>Obed Mitchell</u>
        under Captain Ray, sailing out of Nantucket. He states
        the location in his log as being 30° N. lat. and 174° E.
        long. about halfway between Japan and the Islands.

3.   The names of the ships and their captains are unclear.
        The log of the <u>James Loper</u> does not mention any ships
        with names resembling the ones Jirokichi interpreted.
        According to the log, however, it stated in the item for
        June 18:

> At 10 & 16 [o'clock] spoke with Ship
> Willmington [sic] and Liverpoole [sic] packet
> Cap. Foster and put on board one of the racked
> [wrecked] men.

        In the entry dated July 5 it states:

> Spoke the Massachusetts of New Bedford and
> the Obed Mitchell of Nantucket.

        On the 15th of July it was written:

> Spoke with Ship Nassau of New Bedford.

4.   It was not an accepted practice for Japanese Buddhists
        of this period to eat animal flesh. Consequently, even
        though they may have been starving, the drifters
        usually found it repulsive to eat meat. In view of this,

it is surprising that Jirokichi found the pork to be so delicious.

5.   According to Mr. Edouard A. Stackpole, a noted historian at the Peter Foulger Museum in Nantucket, there was an area on the island that was inhabited exclusively by blacks, called "New Guinea." They were mostly runaway slaves from Maryland or the Norfolk, Virginia area. These men often took jobs on whaling ships.

6.   This was live oak (<u>Quercus virginiana</u>), a wood of great tensile strength and resistance to rot. Its naturally curved limbs made it ideal for ship construction. Thousands of men went south from New England to work in live-oak forests during the winters. These men were called "live-oakers." They felled the timber and hewed it into proper shape, then lugged the pieces which weighed tons from the hummocks to coastal landings where schooners were waiting to carry them north to shipyards.

7.   Koga put all of Jirokichi's descriptions of western-style ships together in one chapter, so it is impossible to determine which ship he was describing--American, English or Russian. In this book the descriptions have been separated by context wherever possible.

8.   According to Alexander Starbuck in <u>History of the American Whale Fishery</u>, pp. 346-47, this voyage of the <u>James Loper</u> lasted from June 26, 1838 to May 11, 1842. They returned with 1842 barrels of sperm oil.

NOTES

Chapter III

1.   The Chinese immigrants to the Sandwich Islands were mostly from the Pearl River delta area of South China

which included Canton, Macao and Hong Kong and are usually referred to as "Cantonese" in the text.

2.   Chinese characters are used in Japanese writing along with the Japanese syllabary systems (<u>hiragana</u> and <u>katakana</u>), so Chinese and Japanese people can make themselves understood to some extent by writing. It is somewhat puzzling as to why Captain Heishiro said they hailed from Nagasaki. It may have been because he thought that might be the only Japanese place familiar to the Chinese.

3.   Glass windows, as well as anything made of glass, were especially impressive to the Japanese drifters. Glass was rare in their country at this time.

4.   This couple was probably Rev. and Mrs. Titus Coan. Coan, a graduate of Auburn Theological Seminary in Massachusetts, sailed from Boston in December, 1834. Stationed in Hilo and Puna, he was pastor of the Haili Church in Hilo until his death in December, 1882.

5.   The Japanese showed much curiosity about this repulsive custom. They were to learn more about it later in the narrative. As for extracting the teeth to prevent the theft of sugar cane, it is hard to believe.

6.   Rev. Dwight Baldwin was a graduate of Yale University and Auburn Theological Seminary. He also attended medical lectures at Harvard. Baldwin sailed from New Bedford, Massachusetts, on Dec. 28, 1830 on the <u>New England</u>. He was at Lahaina on Maui Island from 1835 to 1870 where he served as pastor and educator. For more details on his colorful life see <u>Dr. Baldwin of Lahaina</u> by Mary Charlotte Alexander, Berkeley, Calif. 1953.

In an early newspaper published in the Sandwich Islands called <u>The Polynesian</u>, dated October 17, 1840, the entire first page is devoted to Rev. Baldwin's explanation of the Japanese numerical system.

The following is a lengthy description of the Japanese visitors by Rev. Baldwin as published in The Polynesian, August 1, 1840, pp. 30-31. In view of the scarcity of any material published about the drifters in Western publications, and because of the candid and engaging point of view of the author upon meeting the first Japanese of his experience, I will include the article "Shipwrecked Japanese" in its entirety.

> Having been requested to prepare some account of the unfortunate Japanese who were driven in a gale from their own country and brought to these islands in the fall of 1839, I will attempt to comply, though I have to regret that I have but few facts at command respecting them, and these mostly of a general character. This scarcity of facts is owing to two causes: 1. The imperfect medium of communication while these men were with me; and 2. It did not occur to me, that, it would devolve on me to give an account of them to the public. Still I think, I have the general outline of their history and what has befallen them; and can give it with some degree of accuracy. This work I shall do most cheerfully, if I can hereby subserve the cause of humanity by conferring a favor on these unfortunates.
>
> I would just remark here, that where I shall try to express Japanese names by English letters, the vowels will generally have the sound which they have in European languages; i.e. a in name or e in met; i as i in machine; o is both long and short; and u does not differ from the general sound of the same letter in English. In pronouncing words of two syllables, they generally accent the last but one. In this respect, they doubtless resemble the Chinese and perhaps other neighboring countries.

"Shipwrecked Japanese"

My first interview with the three Japanese was
on the 18th of October, 1839. I had been absent
from my dwelling, and on returning perceived a
crowd in the house and about the door. On
entering I had not time to learn the cause which
had drawn them together, when I saw the three
men, of the general appearance of the Chinese,
but more tawny, sitting before me, apparently in
a humble posture, and bowing still more
humbly; each, at every bow, carrying both hands
over his knees till he touched his feet. These
bows were often repeated. Who are these
visitors? I inquired; and was soon informed by
Capt. Cathcart of the whaleship James Loper,
who was present, that they were three of seven
Japanese, whom he had taken from the wreck of
a large junk of perhaps 150 or 200 tons, on the
6th of June. The other four had been disposed
of on board other whaleships which were to
land them at Oahu. Capt. Cathcart had kindly
taken care of these and supplied all their wants
for four months and a half, and now wished to
leave them at this place.

From the log book of the Obed Mitchell, a ship
which was near when the James Loper fell in
with the unfortunate wreck, by the kindness of
Capt. Ray, I learned more definitely of the
place where they met with them. It was in
north latitude 30 degrees, and east longitude 174
degrees, about half way between the Islands of
Japan and the Sandwich Islands. When all their
movable property was transferred to the
whaleship, the junk was set on fire, and it is
due to the kindness and generosity of Capt.
Cathcart, a generosity often met with among
seafaring men, to state, that not only were these
sufferers provided with food and necessary
clothing, but so far as I could learn, were
landed here with all the movable property they

had saved, including a considerable amount of
money, gold and silver, coined in shape of
parallelograms, all which, on their escaping the
wreck, was put in the care of Capt. Cathcart,
but none was reserved by way of compensation.

I had never before seen a Japanese. Such was
the case with most who were present. Of course
the sight of these men awakened no little
curiosity. We wished to know what strange
events had befallen them; and to learn some
thing about their country for which the people
of all nations were effectually excluded. I
addressed them in English; but though they had
been four and a half months on board the ship,
they had picked up little of our tongue. Others
spoke to them in Hawaiian--the first time, of
course, that they had heard such sounds; others
talked loud that they might overcome what
seemed like deafness. Having understood,
however, that the written languages of the
Chinese and Japanese were the same, we called
in the aid of a Chinaman who could speak some
English and who carried on conversation with
them, with as profound silence as the deaf and
dumb do their intercourse. He wrote our
interrogatories, which the oldest of the Japanese
read carefully, and occasionally with much
hesitation, and then wrote his reply. Many of
the written characters are the same in both
nations; and each nation has many that are
peculiar to itself. Still each may perhaps
understand some of the characters peculiar to
the other. The Japanese and the Chinese like
the Hebrews, in their writing and printing,
begin at the last end of the book, and turn back
to what an Englishman would call the
beginning. The Hebrews, however, write their
lines horizontally, while the Chinese and
Japanese proceed to perpendicular lines from
the top to the bottom. The amount of
information, however, gained from this

interview, respecting these men, was small. I
learned more by incidental and repeated
conversations afterward.

The oldest of these men, by the name of
Heshero, was called among them, "the old man".
He might be fifty years of age, was of spare
habit, and rather small in stature. He was by
far the most manly character among them, and
appeared to be very kind and conscientious. He
had attended most to the schools of their
country, was probably the most skilled in their
written language, and was always employed
with writing with a brush and India ink, except
when he could do something to make himself
useful to us. He had, doubtless, been a model of
industry. He seemed also to be the most devoted
to the idolatry of his country---had an idol,
which was nothing more then a gilded human
figure on a cloth like velvet. This was rolled up
and enclosed, with a string of beads, in a
wooden boxes which was sometimes hung up in
the apartment they occupied---sometimes in our
house; and from its being missing at certain
seasons, we presume he paid his adorations to it
every day. Any thing else he had he seemed
ready to part with; but when sometimes we
intimated that this would be a fine curiosity to
send to America, he would clasp his hands to his
breast, shake his head, and say, "By by me die."
He was the owner of the junk; and had, it was
said, one or two more vessels in his own
country, and one on the stocks, and was
probably wealthy. He had a wife and five
children. When first received on board the
whale ship, he paid to the other six men all that
was due them. In doing this, a dispute arose
among them, whether they should receive pay
up to the time when they left the junk, or only
to the time when it was disabled in the gale,
and driven from their coast. The matter was
referred to Capt. Cathcart for decision.

The second of the three, was probably about twenty-five or thirty years of age, for I do not recollect how old he called himself. He was a man of middling stature, but exceedingly muscular, as may be judged by the fact, that he has more than once of his own accord been down to the beach, and taken a barrel of flour on his shoulders, brought it up with perfect ease, and set it down upon the floor, with as much steadiness as any man could set down a pound's weight. He was employed probably as clerk of the junk; he was pretty well versed in writing, and had some skill in drawing. His name was Ijero [Jirokichi]. In some respects he was more intelligent than the old man; and being much more ready in catching up both the Hawaiian and English languages, it was from him that most of my information was obtained.

The third, named Kinsiu (Kinzo], about sixteen or seventeen years of age, was generally silent and sedate in his appearance for a boy; but was, in every respect, a boy seemingly disposed to nothing but to spend his time in idleness.

When these Japanese were first landed here they went to live with a chinaman; but becoming dissatisfied, they came to our house, in a day or two, with all their effects, consisting of an iron bound box or two, several basket trunks, a pretty good supply of clothing and a bag of money, which belonged to the old man. From the first, from the necessity of the case or from some other cause, they showed the most entire confidence in us, leaving their money or other effects with us, apparently without the least fear of being defrauded.

During the few weeks spent at our house their great object was to obtain a passage to Oahu; hoping some vessel would take them to Canton, whence they thought they could make their way by land to Japan. Their desires on this subject were intense. Whenever a vessel of any description anchored in our roads, they would come to me saying, "schooner," or "feni (vessel) go Oahu." The earnestness of the old man, on such occasions, was beyond description. As he bowed down humbly before us, he would point to our children and say kudomo (Japanese boy) and at the same time hold up five fingers, meaning he had five children in Japan; with the other hand, he would point to his eye, saying "me no see," with an eloquence of expression to be fully understood by no one but the tender hearted parent. After a few weeks they obtained passage to Oahu, where, I am sorry to add in two or three days after their arrival, the old man, after a sick and painful night, was found dead in the morning. He was buried at Honolulu.

After a short time, no vessel offering for China, Ijero returned to this place, accompanied by the three who had been originally landed at Oahu, named respectively Roqf, [Rokubei] (Japanese six) Shetz, [Shichizaemon] (seven) and Hach [Hachizaemon] (eight). As Ijero and one of the three men spent a longer time with our family, I occasionally improved the opportunity to learn more respecting them, their language, their religion and their country. Communications were, as already stated, at first, very limited and difficult, but as they gradually came to understand some English and Hawaiian words, and I learned some Japanese terms, we found it easy to make each other understood, on any except abstract subjects.

The following are important items of information respecting this unfortunate company. The name of their vessel or junk, was Choajamur [Chojamaru]. Both the vessel and the owner, as well as all the crew, belonged to a

place called Iko (Ecchu); or as Ijero sometimes
spoke of it Iko no guinye [Ecchu no kuni -
Ecchu province] what the addition of the last
part signifies I am unable to say. This place is
on the island of Nipon [sic] the largest of the
Japan islands; is situated on some part of the
bay on the west side of the island which is laid
down about half way between the northern and
so extremities. It is nearly opposite from Jedo,
the capital, and probably about in a northwest
direction from it. They say that Iko is one
hundred miles from Jedo, and it takes from ten
days to travel it on foot. Its situation may be
known by that of the island of Sodo [Sado]
which is north of the above mentioned bay, and
is seventy miles, or one day's sail from Iko. The
island of Sodo abounds in gold and silver.

The Chojamaru was engaged, it seems, in the
coasting trade. They had on board rice, an
intoxicating liquor made of rice, and dried fish.
They had proceeded up the western coast of
Nipon, and passed through the straits on the
north of the island, i.e. between Nipon and the
island of Iesso [Ezo], or Matsmai [Matsumai].
Here they were overtaken by a violent gale from
the west, which drove them into the Pacific, out
of sight of land, and dismasted their vessel,
leaving them but a wreck. The hull of their
vessel does not, however, seem to have been
greatly injured, or at least, was not very leaky
afterwards. They must have known pretty well
the direction of the land after the gale, as the
old man had a small compass, which he ordered
to be brought to me after his death. They had
also contrived to erect something like a jurymast
in order to manage the vessel. But owing,
probably to the insufficiency of their spars and
rigging, to the unfavorable winds, and frequent
western blows which prevail in that part of the
ocean, during winter, they were unable to make
the island again; but continued to be driven

farther and farther east. It must have been about the first of January, 1839, that they met with their first disaster; as they were floating in this sad condition for five long and weary months, until they fell in with the James Loper, on the sixth of June following, about half way from Nipon to the Sandwich Islands. A short time before they fell in with this ship, their supply of water failed, and six days they were without any thing to drink, watching the heavens for signs of rain. Their rice was gone, and nothing but their fish remained. All their number, which was ten at the commencement of their voyage, had survived all hardships, till this overtook them. Their sufferings, during this period of thirst, were intense. They speak of putting pieces of silver into their mouths to cool their parched tongues. Three of the ten died during this period; and the remaining seven were reduced to such weakness that not one of them, no not even the sturdy Ijero, could stand alone, or do any thing but crawl about the deck. At the end of six days, they were relieved by a fall of rain which they caught, at first in their hands; and afterwards in such containers as they had. This furnished them a supply till they were taken from the wreck. These are the most important particulars which occur to me now respecting the disaster.

There are many interesting items which I gathered respecting their country. One is, they themselves know nothing of the name Japan, by which we designate their islands. Their largest island they call Nipon, accenting the last syllable. The island north they usually call Matsmai, but are acquainted with the name of Iesso [Ezo]. The place on Kiusiu [Kyushu] at the south where the Dutch are allowed to trade, which is called on all our maps, Nangasaki [Nagasaki], they call only by name of Nanasig, accenting the second syllable. There is a place, probably in Corea, where many of the Niponese junks go to trade, which they call Chusing [Chosen] which is two days sail from Nipon.

Another item of information I learned is, that a very great proportion of the people of these islands are given to excessive intemperance. They say, they do business in the forenoon, and lie drunk the rest of the day. The liquor they use is made by the fermentation of rice, in immense cisterns made for the purpose. The process for making it, I believe, is generally, if not always, by fermentation only, without distillation.

On being asked what their food was in Nipon, they replied, "All the people eat rice for breakfast, rice for dinner, rice for supper, rice to day, rice to morrow, rice next day, and rice every day." Fish is generally used, animals though plenty, are not eaten.

The most interesting item to me of all which I learned from these men was their system of numerals, an abstract of which I might, hereafter give for your paper, if desired. I copied their numerals up to <u>eighty</u> one places of decimals as expressed by our figures; and yet, what is truly wonderful, this immense number is expressed, by them by the combination of only eighteen different words.

Of their system of idolatry I learned but little. They had some books with them, which treated of their religion. They said, they had five principal gods in Nipon, and a multitude of inferior ones. While they were with us, I tried every expedient to interest them in the Christian religion, but probably without much success. They often attended our meetings, at which they appeared attentive and thoughtful but after a conversation on the subject, Ijero, would generally say, "the God of Americans is good for Americans; and our gods are good for us."

The six surviving Niponese are now at Oahu, waiting anxiously for some opportunity that shall convey them towards their home. Some of them have wives and children there, and all of them friends whose looks are as fresh in their minds as though they had left them but yesterday; and they long to meet them again. They might possibly reach Nipon by way of Canton; and perhaps by the way of Kamchatka. Any merchant vessel, or vessel of war, which can aid them in their return, will not only confer a favor on them, but on all who love the cause of humanity.

> Yours truly,
> D. Baldwin

NOTES

Chapter IV

1.   The Polynesian dated June 6, 1840 included an item about the arrival of the Japanese in Honolulu:

> There are in the town, under the care of Dr. Judd, four Japanese who were taken by a whaleship from the wreck of a junk, on which they had been driven about by wind and wave, for many months and suffered great hardships. Their story is full of interest, and which we hope to receive for a future number from Dr. Baldwin of Maui, in whose family the most intelligent of the number has resided for some time. [This was Jirokichi.]

Levi Chamberlain, accountant and Superintendent of Secular Affairs for the mission in Oahu also wrote about it in his journal, pp. 44-47, Vol. 23:

> Saturday Novr 2nd 1839... In the same vessel (The <u>Paalua</u>) came down three Japanese who were in connection with four others picked up at sea on board a junk by the <u>Jas. Loper</u>, Cap. Cathcart. The four arrived at this place some time ago having been put on bd. another vessel at sea by Cap. Cathcart. The <u>three</u> who were landed at Lahaina being strongly recommended to our attention by Mr. Baldwin, we have taken in and afforded them accommodation in the dobie house built by Mr. Parker for his accommodation during gen. meeting.

Chamberlain, an unmarried member of the second group of missionaries to arrive in the Islands, sailed from New Haven, Connecticut in Nov. 1822. A very highly respected member of the community, he tirelessly served as a circuit teacher on Oahu, as well as kept books for the mission.

2.   Rev. Hiram Bingham (1789-1869) and his wife came to the Islands with the first group of missionaries from New England, arriving April 4, 1820. He was the founder and architect of the Kawaiahao Church in Honolulu which was being built when the <u>Chojamaru</u> drifters were there. Bingham also translated portions of the Bible as well as Christian hymns into the Hawaiian language. A man of versatile talents and great energy we can very well call him the "Father of the Missionary Movement" in the Islands.

After serving twenty tempestuous years in the Islands he and his family returned to New England on August 3, 1840 because of his wife's failing health.

His son, Hiram Bingham Jr. returned to Hawaii in 1857. Hiram Bingham III was born in Honolulu in 1875. He is famous for having discovered the ruins of Machu Picchu in Peru in 1911.

For more details on Rev. Bingham's life see <u>A Residence of Twenty-One Years in the Sandwich</u>

<u>Islands</u> by Rev. Hiram Bingham, Hezekiah Huntington, New York, 1848. Republished by Chas. E. Tuttle Co.

Dr. Gerrit P. Judd was born in Paris Hill, New York in 1803. In 1828 he came to the Islands with his wife to serve as a medical missionary for the Presbyterian Church. Dr. Judd figures prominently in several drifting stories, aiding the men with medical attention and in many other ways.

3.   This was King Kamehameha III (1825-54). Unfortunately Jirokichi dismisses this important occasion with just a few laconic sentences about the king.

4.   An item in the journal of Levi Chamberlain dated Nov. 5, 1839, gives more insights into the circumstances of the death of Captain Heishiro:

> Tuesday Novr. 5 1839. This morning George [?] informed me that one of the Japanese which we have lodged was unwell. That he had been ill according to the testimony of his companions during the night in consequence of which they had all been deprived of rest. And that they did not wish to be disturbed to receive food. Hearing that the old man was sick I directed George to inform Dr. Judd which he immediately went to do, but failed to find him. About noon he went again to the house where the men were lodged and now found to his surprise that the man was dead and from the fact of his body's being perfectly cold it was judged that he had been dead for some time. As soon as I had received this information I requested George to give notice to the Dr. that he might examine the corpse, which was done. From the account of the case given by the two companions of the deceased it was concluded that the disease was cramp or inflammation of the bowels, as the signs given implied that the seat of the pain was the bowels & stomach. The

man did not appear to be aware that their
companion was dead till George called about
noon to arouse them. When on uncovering him
supposing him only to be asleep he was found
stiff and cold, they were much affected and
bowing their heads low they wept with many
tears; but made no noise.

The other f̲o̲u̲r̲ who had been their fellow
sufferers in the junk and with them rescued
from the jaws of a lingering death to which
they were exposed in their wrecked condition,
were made acquainted with the melancholy fact
and came to mingle their tears and perform
superstitious ceremonies over the body of their
companion and commander, as the deceased was
owner of the wrecked vessel.

I gave directions to have a coffin made and
pointed out a spot in the burying ground where
his body might be interred---for these attentions
they seemed to be grateful. And desirous that
the interment soon take place. It was thought
best to delay it however until tomorrow, as the
time for doing all the work was short, and it
seemed also proper that as the death was so
sudden and happening in such circumstances,
the body should be further examined; which was
done in the evening by Dr. Judd. The King also
calling at the house to observe the strangers in
their grief. No suspicions were entertained by
Dr. Judd of any unfairness in relation to the
cause of the death; on the contrary it was
regarded by him as one of those visitations of
providence around which a veil is drawn by him
who doeth his own will & giveth no account of
his matters.

Chamberlain continues the following day:

Wednesday Novr. 6, 1839. The interment of the
stranger took place in the common burying

ground. Quite a number of natives, church members & others collected around the house where the remains were laying decently enclosed in a coffin; which when placed in a cart were drawn to the grave followed by the Japanese as mourners & by the natives who fell in behind. At the grave Mr. Bingham read a portion of Scripture & offered a prayer part in native & part in English.

The mans name as communicated by Mr. Baldwin is "Heshero." He left a wife and children in Japan---three sons and two daughters ---his desire to return was very strong. Alas! he has gone to his long home and will never see again in the flesh the faces of those he seemed so much to love. And they---long since probably have ceased to expect his return, or if the hope of it has at any time lighted up a feeling of joy in the bosom of the desolate mother it was but for a moment:---and the chilling uncertainty of his fate has again frozen her joy.

5. The stone monument was evidently never placed on Captain Heishiro's grave in Kawaiahao Cemetery behind the church. Today there is no marker, only stones for Rev. Bingham's children.

6. See Note 10, Introduction, about this party of drifters.

7. The characters used in Japanese for the United States are pronounced bei-koku or "rice country."

8. In Tokei Monogatari the words "merashi tobacco" are written murashi-shi tabaka. It probably refers to molasses tobacco.

9. Mexican and Spanish vaqueros (cowboys) were brought to the Sandwich Islands in the 1830's by King Kamehameha III to tame the wild cattle which were destroying crops. At first there were only 12 head of cattle on Oahu Island which were given to the king by

a British captain, but the number increased rapidly. The Hawaiians picked up the cattle-roping skills from the vaqueros.

10.   It is not clear who this "Mr. Barney" was. In an article in The Friend, a Honolulu missions publications, dated April, 1928 titled, "Reminiscences of the Hawaii of Ninety Years Ago By a Shipwrecked Japanese" written by Dr. Harada Rasuku, he says, "The 'guest' (Jirokichi) tells about a large American store kept by Mr. Chamberlain (Levi Chamberlain?) and of his great wealth.   Nevertheless, Mr. Chamberlain was most cordial to the Japanese." I am inclined to think that this "Mr. Barney" and Mr. Chamberlain are the same person.

11.   Sometimes Jirokichi referred to this "John" as Papiyu's brother and at other times as his nephew.   Called "China John" by the missionaries, they were violently opposed to him.   From the journal of Stephen Reynolds, July 28, 1840.

NOTES

Chapter V

1.   This was undoubtedly the Lahaina Middle School which was originally called Lahainaluna Seminary. It was established in 1831 by American missionaries with an enrollment of sixty scholars.

2.   It is unclear what this explosive was, maybe phosphorus.

3.   Japanese drifters were always anxious to get back to their homeland no matter what the circumstances were. Sir George Simpson heard about this when he was in the Sandwich Islands in the course of his circumnavigation of the world and made the following comments in his book:

The people of China...are...ready to go abroad
either as residents or as wanderers, combining
the laborious habits of the Irish with the
peddling disposition of the Jews. In this
respect, they are remarkably different from the
Japanese, who even when they find themselves
from home with hardly the hope of returning
home think of nothing but their native country.

This was eminently the case with the two little
bands (the Chojamaru party and the drifters
from Echigo) that were driven,..to the shores of
this group. Notwithstanding all the kindness
that they experienced, particularly from the
missionaries, they pined for their own islands.
The young as well as the old, the single as well
as the married...

From Narrative of a Journey Around the World by Sir
George Simpson (Governor of the Hudson's Bay
Company) Vol.1, Henry Colburn, London, 1847, pp. 151-
52.

4.   It is not clear to what island Jirokichi is referring to
here. From looking at a map they must have seen
Lanai and Kahoolawe Islands.

5.   This French ship was La Danaide. The Polynesian,
August 8, 1840, mentioned this visit:

They (the Japanese) visited La Danaide on
Saturday, where they were politely received by
Capt. Rosamel and shown through the ship. The
complete order and immense power of the
armament seemed to make a deep impression on
their minds.

6.   Oshio Heihachiro (1753-1837) aka Oshio Chusai, was an
idealistic Confucian philosopher and teacher who led
this rebellion in 1837. It was known in Japan as the
"Tempo Uprising" against the Tokugawa government.
It was launched as an action against social injustice of

the downtrodden after a famine had spread in the Kansai district due to a poor rice crop. Oshio and his supporters attacked the shogunate district office in Osaka and set fires in various parts of the city to trigger peasant uprisings.

7.   Just three years before in July, 1837, the Americans attempted to repatriate the three survivors of the Hojunmaru drifting event. (See notes # 3 and 7 of the Introduction). The three men had been taken from the American west coast to China via Europe. After a two-year stay in Macao, this attempt was made to take them home. As soon as the Morrison entered Edo Bay it was hit by cannon fire. Another try was made at Kagoshima, but shogunate officials thwarted that endeavor as well. The drifters lived out their lives in China.

8.   The Bonin Islands (known as Ogasawara Islands in Japan), a group of some thirty islands located about 900 kms. south of Tokyo, were first visited by Occidentals in 1793 when Captain James Magee of the Margaret of Boston "discovered" them. During the first half of the 19th century whalers often stopped there. The first settlers came in 1830 when five Westerners of various nationalities, and 25 Hawaiians, boarded a schooner in Honolulu bound for the islands in May. Contrary to what Jirokichi heard, the main purpose for establishing a settlement there was to provide a base where whalers could replenish their supplies of wood, water and fuel, and serve as a recreation ground for sailors.

The Japanese claimed the islands based on their discovery in 1593 by Ogasawara Sadayori. They remained sparsely populated until the foreign settlers moved there. Perry stopped there on his way to Japan and raised the American flag, but they were formally annexed by the Japanese again in 1880. Captured by the American military in 1945, they were restored to Japan in 1968 and are now under the jurisdiction of the Tokyo government.

9.   In The Polynesian dated August 1, 1840 Rev. Baldwin
        wrote another article to enlighten the local population
        about Japan. It contains sundry information that was
        gleaned from "Izero" (Jirokichi), including something
        about the Christians who came to Japan:

>   "To the above letter [Rev. Baldwin's] we add the
>   following items, collected from Izaro, while in
>   this town." [It starts with a list of retail prices
>   for manufactured goods in Japan which was
>   given as a service to "any enterprising merchant
>   who may make the attempt to open a traffic
>   with that country"...]
>
>   The article continues "Silver bears a much
>   greater value than gold. One ounce being equal
>   to five of silver.
>
>   America is called Augusto.[?]
>
>   Izero says he has read in the books of his
>   country, "Kiriston Shunam padere" [?] that
>   "christians are very bad men." He has as strong
>   an antipathy to the name of christian as the
>   aborigines of America had after the bloody
>   attempts to proselyte them to that faith. He was
>   much astonished to learn that those who had
>   rescued him from shipwreck and had protected
>   him since, called themselves christians. Said it
>   was impossible, "Christians are no good these
>   men are very, very good."
>
>   He also states that a teacher of that religion,
>   whom he calls "padere," probably padre, came to
>   reside at Ktusin, Amasaka. He was at first
>   poor, but having made many converts, obtained
>   great possessions.
>
>   The king hearing of it ordered every vestige of
>   the religion to be destroyed, and compelled the
>   people to trample upon a certain sign they had.
>   He does not know what it was. [This was

undoubtedly a <u>fumi-e</u>, literally a "trampling picture." It had the crucifixion or some other holy image depicted on it.] The priest then encouraged them to keep it in their hearts.

Japanese books represent tropical climates as insupportable. Izero has seen the heat represented by a man standing and pouring water over himself.

Tinshuakoati (the divine sun) name of the present king, or dairi, now in the eleventh year of his reign, lives at Kiuto [Kyoto] near Osaka. Like the sun he cannot be looked at. Iasko Oo, is Diquon or high officer, lives at Jeddo [Edo] and rules the realm.

Tinsh [Tempo] is the name of the present dynasty. Several dialects are used in the country. Written language is uniform throughout the islands.

Murder, theft, arson, kidnapping are punished by beheading. Adultery by three months imprisonment. Polygamy is unlawful, four to six months imprisonment. Deception and some other crimes by flogging. Marriage is contracted by the parents and solemnized by the priest. Osaka was burnt five or six years ago in a civil commotion. Slavery is unknown; also counterfeit money. Izero has handled coin eighteen years and never saw any that was bad...

10. When Jirokichi was young he lived in Matsumae. One time he saw a fleet of nine foreign ships pass through the Tsugaru Straits. In spite of the fact that a hail of projectiles were fired at them from the Japanese side, not one of them hit the target. On the foreign ships they remained so calm that they did not even bother to open their port holes. They moved away from the coast and then shot off one cannon ball that made a direct hit on Matsumae Castle, the headquarters of the

clan. The occupants were in such a state of confusion they didn't know what to do. According to Jirokichi Westerners were so skillful at determining distance that they never missed a shot. (From the notes of the editors of Bandan, pp. 275-76.)

11.   Needless to add, this plan did not materialize when Commodore Perry's Black Ships came to Uraga in 1853 and 1854.

12.   An item in The Polynesian, August 8, 1840, said:

> The Rev. H. Bingham after a residence of 20 years takes the voyage in the Flora on account of the feeble health of Mrs. Bingham and to promote the objects of the mission in the U.S. They will be absent about eighteen months.

13.   Rev. Baldwin comments on the leavetaking of the Japanese in the article in The Polynesian, August 1, 1840.

> The public will be gratified to learn that through the liberality of Mr. H. A. Peirce, of the firm Peirce & Brewer, the Japanese have been offered a passage to Kamschatka in a vessel upon the eve of sailing. Upon arrival there, Mr. Peirce will afford them every possible facility for reaching their native land, and it is hoped that a few months more will see them restored to their families and country. They are themselves sanguine of success in being allowed to enter, but it must be confessed that after the hostile reception of those who went in the Morrison, there is but little chance of a friendly welcome for this party.

Also in The Polynesian, dated August 8, 1840, it said:

> The Japanese went in the Harlequin August 3rd, grateful for the hospitality they received at the islands...It is to be regretted that they left so

soon as they were just beginning to acquire ideas which could not fail to be useful should they return to their native land. They will at least be able to say, that Christians are not such dangerous characters as the Niponese [sic] government suppose them to be, since to them they have been mainly indebted for rescue from starvation or a watery grave, for their support in a foreign land and for their outfit and passage home. The idea that their own government are cruel in their treatment of shipwrecked mariners by inhumanly repelling all who return from a foreign land, seemed to be new to their minds, and the government can be excusable only on the supposition that they believe the earth to be flat and Japan 'somewhere about the centre of it', of course a Junk blown off in a storm could not be long absent before they would arrive at the inevitable conclusion that she must have reached the jumping off place 'whence none return'. Such of their subjects as are brought back in ships they probably regard as runaways attached to foreigners and of course like them to be shut out by force from their country. Izero acknowledged the injustice of the law and promised to do all in his power to correct the erroneous impressions of his government.

In case it is inconvenient for the Gov. of Kamachatka [sic] to return these unfortunate men they will remain on board the Harlequin and be again received at this place, and it is hoped that a vessel may be fitted out in the course of a year for the double purpose of returning them and opening a trade if possible on some part of the coast.

NOTES

Chapter VI

1. It is not certain if Jirokichi is describing the sleeping accommodations and kitchen on the Harlequin or the James Loper here.

2. These islands were probably the Ogasawara Islands. See Note 7 for Chapter V.

3. This same may be Beyajinsu, a wealthy merchant in Petropavlovsk at the time.

4. This episode about the punishing of the male nurse is not related in Bandan. It has been taken from Tokei Monogatari. Jirokichi described the circumstances of the Sandwich Islands in more detail than he did those of Russia.

NOTES

Chapter VII

1. The "Company" refers to the Russian-American Company. In 1781 Grigorii Ivanovich Shelikhov, a fellow merchant, I. L. Golikov, and the latter's nephew, mariner M. S. Golikov, organized a company to exploit islands off Alaska reported to be rich in fur-bearing animals. In 1797 the company acquired the name Russian-American Company.

2. Sir George Simpson describes the company location in his Journey Around the World, pp. 248-49:

    The co's post stands near the end of a tongue of land, about 3/4 of a mile in length and 1/4 of a mile in width, so little elevated above the level of the sea, that, when the southerly wind blows or continues long, the whole is almost sure to be inundated. The town lies about a half mile distant, situated on the left bank of the Kuchtui [river]. ... A more dreary scene can scarcely be conceived. Not a tree, and hardly even a green blade, is to be seen within miles of the town; and in the midst of the disorderly collection of huts is a stagnant marsh, unless when frozen, must be a nursery of all sorts of malaria and pestilence. The climate is at least on a par with the soil. Summer consists of 3 months of damp and chilly weather, during great part of which the snow still covers the hills, and the ice chokes the harbor; and this is succeeded by 9 mon. of dreary winter, in which the cold, unlike that of more inland spots, is as raw as it is intense.

3.   This is probably Lt. Vasilii Stepanovich Zavoiko, who was appointed commandant of the post in 1840. In 1843, he moved the company installation to Aian Bay along the southeast shore of Siberia. This location was more advantageous because ships could enter the harbor under any wind conditions.

4.   Lt. Commander Petr Ivanich served under the illustrious Commander Petr Ricord on the Diana when Takadaya Kahei was taken hostage in revenge for the capture of Commander Golovnin by the Japanese in 1811. Details are stated later. See note # 7.

5.   Sir George Simpson adds the following about Madame Zavoiko:

> Madame Zavoiko contrived to combat circumstances so adverse to horticultural operations in hothouses---flowers, potatoes, cabbage, lettuce and barley.

6.   Also from Sir George Simpson's Journey Around the World, pp. 255-56, we get his impression of the Chojamaru drifters who were in Okhotsk at the same time he was:

At Okhotsk we saw the Japanese, of whom I had
previously heard at the Sandwich Islands. They
were maintained at the expense of the
government and were waiting an opportunity to
return home. Whatever the chapter of accident
might ultimately disclose, there was then no
definite prospect that the unhappy exiles would
ever reach the shores of Japan, or that, even if
they should get that length, they would be
allowed to land. On a former occasion of the
same kind, the sailors, whom the Russians were
restoring to their country, were driven off by
their jealous government, an example which is
not very likely to encourage Russia to repeat the
attempt. The Japanese in question, wretched as
their lot must have been in a strange land, and
under an inhospitable climate, contributed to
make themselves more miserable by disagreeing
with each other; and, on a recent occasion, four
of them had conspired to destroy the fifth,
whom the authorities were obliged to send to
prison, in order to preserve his life.

7.   The most celebrated case in which a Russian was held
captive by the Japanese was that in which the highly
respected Russian naval officer, Commander Vasilii
Golovnin, was seized while carrying out a survey of
the southern Kurile islands in 1811. By flattery, he
was lured away and captured by Japanese soldiers,
bound at the neck and ankles with ropes, and with his
men, was forced to walk across Ezo to Matsumae,
where they were imprisoned.

When Commander Petr Rikord, chief of the Kamchatka
region, came to a port on Kunashiri in the _Diana_ the
following year, he attempted to exchange seven
Japanese who had drifted to Kamchatka for the
Russians held at Matsunae. After several unsuccessful
attempts to make a deal with Japanese officials,
Rikord gave his men orders to seize any Japanese
vessel that came into the harbor. The captain of the
ship which was attacked was taken on board the _Diana_

along with several of his sailors. This captain was a prominent shipowner, Takadaya Kahei. Takadaya was taken to Kamchatka and kept hostage in retaliation for the imprisonment of Golovnin. About a year later, Takadaya was taken to Matsumae and through mediation, Golovnin was freed after having spent nearly two years in confinement. Source: <u>Japan As It Was and Is</u>, Richard Hildreth, pp. 460-80.

8.   Muroran is the name of a town near Lake Toya on the south coast of Ezo. The "Muroran Incident" was a direct result of the rebuff Nikolai Rezanov received when he attempted to bring back a party of Japanese drifters in 1804. Rezanov had been commissioned by Alexander I to take the Japanese to Nagasaki and while he was there to make negotiations for opening trade. Angered at being quickly turned away, Rezanov decided to seek revenge without the sanction of his government. By his order Russian sailors attacked a Japanese village in Ezo, taking loot and killing some local people. The indignation of the Japanese concerning these attacks was behind the capture of Golovnin.

9.   Jirokichi and his comrades were taken from Okhotsk on the Russian-American Company 'brig' <u>Konstantin</u>. Fleet Navigator Lt. Kashevarov (either Ivan or Nikolai) one of at least seven known brothers. They arrived at Sitka on September 15.

NOTES

Chapter VIII

1.   There is a discrepancy in Jirokichi's calculation here. They left Okhotsk in mid-July. In <u>Tokei Monogatari</u> the arrival date was given as one month later. The latter is probably correct.

2. The name "Sitka" comes from "Sheetkah" in the language of the native Tlingits. The official name for the area in Russian was Novoarkhangel'sk [New Archangel]. The English called it Norfolk Sound.

3. Adolph Etolin was actually born in Helsingfors, Finland, but he could speak Swedish and Russian. He was appointed Chief Manager (governor) of the Russian-American Company holdingsin 1840 and served at Sitka until 1846 when he returned to Russia.

4. The original "castle" was built when the first chief of the Russian-American Company, Alexander Baranov, came there. That structure was replaced by the one that the Chojamaru drifters saw.

5. Sir George Simpson in his Journey Around the World speaks of enjoying a hot springs bath twenty miles north of New Archangel.

6. The "Korushi" was Jirokichi's interpretation of the Russian word for the Tlingits in Sitka, "Kolosh." They were considered the most ferocious and savage of the natives on the American west coast. The Kolosh were divided amongst themselves in their feelings toward the Russians. Gov. Etolin was the most successful local administrator in keeping peace with the Kolosh.

7. C. L. Andrews says in Story of Alaska that one of the causes of the native attacks was the Russians taking native women. He also conjectures that they were armed by other nations in competition with the Russians for the fur trade.

8. At this time the Russians were beginning to build steamships for use on the northwest coast of America. This ship with the new-style power would make a big change in fur trading while in competition with the English Hudson's Bay Company. By 1840-41 they had built one large and one small steamship.

9.   The <u>Nikolai I</u> had a 60 hp. engine while that of the <u>Mur</u> was only an 8 hp. The Japanese on the <u>Nikolai I</u> were among the first of their countrymen to be transported on a steamship. From the Introduction of <u>Bandan,</u> p. 17.

10.   The Russians were obviously treating the Japanese visitors with special courtesy with the intention of making a good impression and thereby be admitted into Japan to trade.

NOTES

Chapter IX

1.   Captain Gavrilov was born August 18, 1818, so was 25 when seen by Jirokichi. He became famous for his exploration of the Amur River estuary in Siberia. He had twice visited Etorofu with Captain Rikord.

2.   We must view Jirokichi's generalizations about foreign people with caution while considering the circumstances and his narrow point of view. He met only a smattering of each of the nationalities that he describes. His judgments may have been based to a certain extent on the kindnesses that he received.

3.   Just the year before the Bakufu [Japanese government] issued the so-called "Tempo Shinsui" order easing somewhat the severity of the "Beat Off Foreign Ships" order of 1825. This had decreed that foreign ships should be fired upon and if any foreigners landed, they should be arrested or killed. The new edict approved of supplying foreign ships with food, provisions, firewood and water. This came about as a result of the Opium War and the fear of foreign retaliation.

4.   The Dutch jealously guarded the tenuous hold on trade they enjoyed with the Japanese in Nagasaki and were

always on the alert lest some other country seek to infringe on their trading rights.

5.   The Japanese on this ship were probably afraid to associate with the foreigners on the ship, fearing the wrath of the shogunate officials.

6.   In the Introduction of <u>Bandan</u> the editors comment on Kobayashi's behavior toward the Russians. They remark that he was a low-rank samurai who probably despised those in a lower position. They think Jirokichi interpreted in such a way as to smooth things over. He did not tell the Russians what Kobayashi said about the danger of coming near Japan. This explains the Russian record of the event. The Russian historian named Chevumenfu [phonetic spelling - Tikhmenev] said that Captain Gavrilov described the Japanese official's friendly spirit. He added that if they had needed to, they could have come to Kunashiri, Etorofu or even the Japanese mainland. They would have been welcomed, and anything would have been given to them. This misunderstanding prompted the Russians to approach Japan again in 1845. Captain Gavrilov led an expedition to Etorofu, but again it was fruitless. See: P.A. Tikhmenev, <u>A history of the Russian-American Company</u>, Seattle, 1978, pp. 337-338, translated from the edition of 1861-1863, indicating the favorable but mistaken view acquired by the Russians from the 1843 contact.

Later Kobayashi was punished by the shogunate government for taking charge of the drifters by himself.

APPENDIX

Russian documents dealing with the <u>Chojamaru</u> drifters are as follows:

1)   14 April 1843, Communication #105 Sent:

From: Captain A.K. Etholen, Chief Manager (governor) of Russian America

To: The Commander of the brig <u>Promysel</u>, Ensign, Corps of Navigators

Mr. Gavrilov:

In accordance with Company Order No. 631, 6 May 1842, to me, as Chief Manager expressing the Emperor's wish that six shipwrecked Japanese sent form Okhotsk to Novoarkhangel'sk last year be returned to their homeland on a Company vessel, I have selected for this the brig <u>Promysel</u>, to be under your command, as an experienced, efficient and responsible officer. You will therefore take along on the brig being sent from here to Okhotsk and the Kuriles with cargo and passengers sent for service in Okhotsk, and to the islands of Urup, Simusir and Shumshu, the said six Japanese: Khach, Choo, Izhro, Chinzhro, Shemon and Ruksabro. As soon as the brig is ready to put to sea, you are to head directly from this port to the Japanese coasts, to the bay of Atkiz on the island of Matsmai. There you will put the Japanese ashore in two entirely safe small boats prepared here for this, in each of which you are to place in comfort three Japanese with all their baggage, or if the wind and other conditions favor it, you can do this at the village of Urbich in the bay of Sano on the island of Iturup, where in 1836 several shipwrecked Japanese were landed from the boat <u>Unalashka</u> under command of sub-lieutenant (<u>podporuchik</u>) Orlov. Neither there nor anythwere else are you to approach the shore, but instead you are to hold off a safe distance away, out of cannon shot, so as not to subject the vessel and crew to any sort of danger form unfriendly acts of the Japanese inhabitants, as they displayed toward Mr. Orlov. I also enclose for your information, a copy of his report and also you are to be supplied with all necessary maps.

In fulfilling this order you are to follow exactly the rules of the Asiatic Committee, confirmed by the Emperor on 19 November 1835, a copy of which is enclosed. If upon landing there or elsewhere when you are near the Japanese coasts, you observe that some of the inhabitants wish to communicate with you, you are to receive them nicely and in friendly fashion in accordance with the rules, but you are not to enter into any sort of official relations with them and if possible you are to explain to them that your visit to their borders is inspired by the philanthropic intention to return their fellow-countrymen who had suffered shipwreck, and that we do this without an ulterior motive but solely from good feeling toward the Japanese as our nearest neighbors. However, in doing this you are to observe extreme caution so as not to subject the brig and crew to any sort of danger from cunning designs of the Japanese.

As you yourself can testify, the Japanese sent with you have lived comfortably and quietly, at company expense, and have been supplied by the Company with everything necessary for the journey. I therefore ask that during the voyage you also behave as nicely toward them as we have got along with them here, not using them for work, and taking along on the brig an apprentice physician who is going to Okhotsk, who can if necessary give them medical attention, and on sending them from the brig order that they be given all their property, which is to be set safely on shore with them. You are then to leave the Japanese coast at once and continue to the Kuriles and farther, to fulfill my other orders.

In carrying out the Imperial wish that these Japanese be returned to their homeland, you are to obeserve extreme caution and good sense in fulfilling the task which I have entrusted to you, so that it can be fulfilled successfully with praise and to your honor.

From Mr. Orlov's report you will see that it was then observed that there were no sea otters on the northwest side of the island of Iturup; therefore if it is convenient to land the Japanese on the island of Matsmai in the Bay of Atkiz, when enroute to the island of Urup you are to examine the NE side of Iturup to see whether there are any sea otters there. However, do so only after you have landed the Japanese, and not while they are still on the vessel, and only at such a distance from the shore as not to arouse suspicion among the Japanese, who are mistrustful and hostile toward foreigners, nor to expose yourself to any sort of danger.

2) The Russian-American Company Annual Report (otchet) to Shareholders, dated 1 January 1843 (for 1842, p. 46):

"On taking six Japanese to their homeland."

In 1841 six shipwrecked Japanese were taken from Petropavlovsk to Okhotsk on an American vessel. Upon hearing the report of the Vice-Chancellor about this the Sovereign Emperor deigned to order that the Japanese be sent to their homeland by the Russian-American Company or some other means. On 4 May 1842 the naval Ministry transmitted this Sovereign command to the Main Administration [of the colonies], for proper execution. It was therefore ordered that the said Japanese be sent to Sitkha, which was done in August 1842 on the Company brig Konstantin, and the Chief Manager of the colonies was entrusted with execution of the supreme order. The present [Chief Manager], Captain of 1st rank Etolin, reports that the Japanese were housed, clothed and kept at Company expense, and that during their entire stay in Novoarkhangel'sk conducted themselves quietly and modestly, evidently fully aware of the generous treatment accorded them, and upon departure expressed their lively thanks to the Chief Manager. The Company brig Promysel, under command of Ensign of the Navigators Corps Gavrilov, a trustworthy and careful officer was assigned to carry the Japanese to their homeland. The brig left Novoarkhangel'sk on 20 April 1843, and according to information received on 13 October last, successfully fulfilled its task.

BIBLIOGRAPHY

1. *Books in English*

Alexander, Mary C., Dr. Baldwin of Lahaina. Berkeley, CA, 1953.

Andrews, C.L., Story of Alaska. Caxton Printers Ltd., Caldwell, Idaho, 1944

Belcher, Sir Edward. Narrative of a Voyage Around the World, 1836-42. Vol.I., Henry Colburn, London, 1843.

Bingham, Rev. Hiram. A Residence of 21 Years in the Sandwich Islands. Hezekiah Huntington, New Yrok, 1848. Republished by Chas. E. Tuttle Co., 1981.

Chevigny, Hector. Russian America---The Great Alaskan Venture, 1741-1861. Viking Press, New York, 1965.

Delano, Amasa. Narratives of Voyages and Travels. Boston, 1817.

Golovnin, Vasilii M. Memoirs of a Captivity in Japan. London, 1824.

Hildreth, Richard. Japan As It Was and Is. Boston: Phillips Sampson & Co., 1855.

Lensen, George Alexander. The Russian Push Toward Japan. Princeton University Press, 1959.

Plummer, Katherine. The Shogun's Reluctant Ambassadors. Lotus Press, Tokyo, 1984.

Sakamaki, Shunzo. Japan and the United States, 1790-1854. Scholarly Resources, Inc., Wilmington, Delaware, 1973.

Simpson, Sir George. Narrative of A Journey Around the World. Vol.I, Henry Colburn, London, 1847.

Starbuck, Alexander. History of the American Whale Fishery. Waltham, Mass., 1878.

Wildes, Harry Emerson. Aliens in the East. Scholarly Resources, Inc., Wilmington, Delaware, 1973.

2.   *Books in Japanese*

Endo, Takanori. Tokei Monogatari (in Nihon Shomin Seikatsu Shiryo Shusei), Sanichi Shobo, Tokyo, 1968, Vol.5.

Koga, Kinichiro. Bandan. Edited by Yamori, Kazuhiko and Muroga Nobuo Heibonsha, Tokyo, 1965.

Takase, Shigeo. Chojamaru no Hyoryu. Shimizu Shoin, Tokyo, 1974.

3.   *Magazines, Periodicals and Journals*

The Levi Chamberlain Journal, Mission Children's Society Library, Honolulu, Vol.23, Nov, 2, 5, 6, 1839.

The Friend, Honolulu, april, 1928.

The Hawaiian Spectator, Vol.I, No. 3, July 1938.

Papers of the Hawaiian Historical Society, No. 18, October, 1931.

The Mid-Pacific, Honolulu, Vol.41, January 1931.

The Polynesian, Honolulu, June 6, 1840; Aug. 1, 8, 17, 1840.

The Stephen Reynolds Journal, Mission Children's Society Library, Honolulu, July 28, 1840.

INDEX

ILLUSTRATIONS

I. WRECK AND RESCUE; LIFE ON A WHALER

1. Jirokichi, from a sketch by the son of Koga Kinichiro, the author of <u>Bandan</u>.

2. Awaiting death.

3. Kinroku begging Kinzo for water. Deliverance: the <u>James Loper</u> on the horizon.

4. Captain Obed Cathcart. The whaler <u>James Loper</u>.

5. Climbing aloft. Sighting a whale. Whaleboats in pursuit.

6. The harpooner. Ready to "cut in," with a cutting spade. Getting the whale alongside (two blubber hooks hang over the side.)

7. Bailing spermaceti from the "case" of a sperm whale. Whaling operations aboard the <u>James Loper</u>. A harpoon.

8. The crewman Anthony. Food on the whaler - probably ship's bread and hash or lobscouse. Construction of the crow's nest. The ship's bell.

9. A windlass for raising anchors, and on whaleships for raising blubber from whales during cutting-in process.

10. Anchors, with wooden and iron stocks. Blubber hook. Speaking trumpet.

11. Grindstone for sharpening harpoons, lances, cutting spades. Tryworks for rendering oil from blubber.

12. Mincing knife for scoring blubber before trying out. Harpoons. A line tub for storing harpoon line. Boarding knife for severing large pieces of blubber.

Cutting spade for cutting-in whales. Pump. Casks for whale oil.

13.   A cooling vat, for cooling oil before storage in casks. Deck scrubbing equipment.

II.   THE SANDWICH (HAWAIIAN ISLANDS)

14.   Wailuku port on Maui Island. Wailuku beach area, showing the local magistrate's house, church, ntavie huts, and sugar press.

15.   Furnishings in Rev. Baldwin's house, Lahaina; fireplace; bellows; doorknob; cooking implements (length, left & right 2', 1', 2', 1.5"); and range.

16.   Hawaii Island: Hilo harbor and volcano. The residence of the Chinese in Hilo.

17.   Mauna Loa volcano from Hilo. Arrival at Honolulu.

18.   Two views of Oahu harbor at Honolulu: the King's Palace may be seen on the right, in enclosure; Rev. Bingham's house; four churches in one area, two piers, three breakwaters, a salt manufacturing place, the slaughtering hut (near breakwater on the left), and the homes of the butchers and slaughterers.

19.   Rev. Bingham. Rev. and Mrs. Bingham going to church. Captin Heishiro's grave marker; flowers of the plant that Rev. Bingham planted on the grave; and the fence around the grave.

20.   King Hamehameha III and the view from the Palace. The flag and the Palace grounds.

21.   Native men and women on Oahu Island.

22.   A Bengali man; a Frenchman; a Spaniard; and a Black man, playing the fiddle.

23. American's residences. Harbor entrance (on the right), the morning marketplace, and huts for natives and servants.

24. Papiyo, dressed to go out, and at home. His store.

25. Papiyo's house; and entrance. A Cantonese with a watch. A lantern, showing the spring device.

26. Taro, and utensils for making poi. A vendor selling poi.

27. A cotton plant. Breadfruit and tree; maina (cotton).

28. A tobacco case; mortar and pestle for grinding tobacco; rolled tobacco. Pepperberries and leaf. A cattle pen on a ranch.

29. Taking a cow to the slaughterhouse.

30. The slaughterhouse and the storehouse for hides, showing hides drying on the beach. Right: the slaughterhouse, showing cow tied up outside. The carcass ahnging from a beam, and a diagram of the floor, showing the openings for the blood to flow through to the sea.

31. Sugar manufacturing: a sprig of sugar cane. Implements for making rock sugar. Cauldron for boiling the juice.

32. Sugar manufacturing.

33. Sugar manufacturing: The stone troughs and funnel-shaped posts. Transporting the sugar.

34. Printing. The printing press, showing the roller for applying the ink. The stone place for making engravings; the cover and stand are of wood. Pens and ink. A slate and writing implement.

35. Ship repair facilities: the slip in Honolulu; T-shaped loading dock.

36. A missionary school, Oahu, with cooling device attached to the exterior, consisting of a cotton sail and wooden pole. When the wood blew through the bag it wade it cool. Also used on ships. A close-up of the cooling device. A cooling shelf beside the house, 11 meters high and 3 meters square.

37. Windmill and pump. On left side of the roof of the building a "cooling shelf."

38. Salt manufacturing implements and sacks. The salt beach on Lanai Island.

39. Preparations for making an adobe wall. Men and women riding bareback.

40. Catching a wild boar. Horse with saddle. Riding a tortoise.

41. Rev. Bingham's leavetaking on the Flora.

III. PETROPAVLOVSK, KAMCHATKA

42. Captains Sen and Carter. Sleeping quarters aboard ship.

43. Petropavlovsk. Kamchatka Harbor.

44. The hospital at Petropavlovsk.

45. Kamchatka house; dogs chained up; going for firewood.

46. Petropavlovsk society.

47. A wedding. Measuring a man's height.

48. The flogging of a male nurse (from Tokei Monogatari). Winter sports.

49.   Hunting scenes.

50.   A Petropavlovsk dwelling. Killing a goat.

51.   Bedroom furnishings (cloth hanging in doorway).

IV.   OKHOTSK

52.   Okhotsk settlement and harbor.

53.   Commandant's house. On right, flag of the Russian-American Company.

54.   Hothouse. Plant. Stove.

55.   Stoves.

56.   Commandant, at home and in uniform. Commandant's daughter, showing types of hair arrangements.

57.   Feminine styles.

58.   Feminine styles.

59.   Transport.

60.   Tungus people. Dog. Street Scene.

61.   Eating utensils. Towel or napkin.

62.   Soldier receiving beating. Fettered malefactor at work. Another, with nose cut off.

63.   Troops and weapons.

64.   Troops and weapons.

65.   Weapons. Rifles in rack.

66.   Countryside near Okhotsk. Commandant and wife on journey.

1.   *Jirokichi, from a sketch by the son of Koga Kinichiro, the author of <u>Bandan</u>. The <u>Chojamaru</u>*

2.   *Awaiting death.*

3.   *Kinroku begging Kinzo for water. Deliverance: the*
James Loper on the horizon.

4. *Captain Obed Cathcart. The whaler <u>James Loper</u>.*

5.   *Climbing aloft. Sighting a whale. Whaleboats in pursuit.*

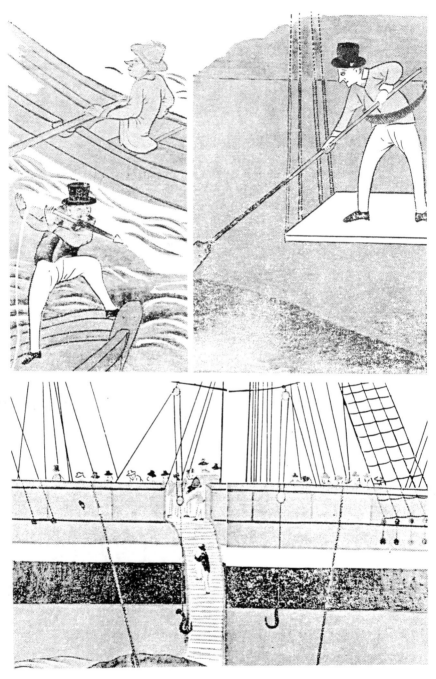

6.   The harpooner. Ready to "cut in," with a cutting spade. Getting the whale alongside (two blubber hooks hang over the side.)

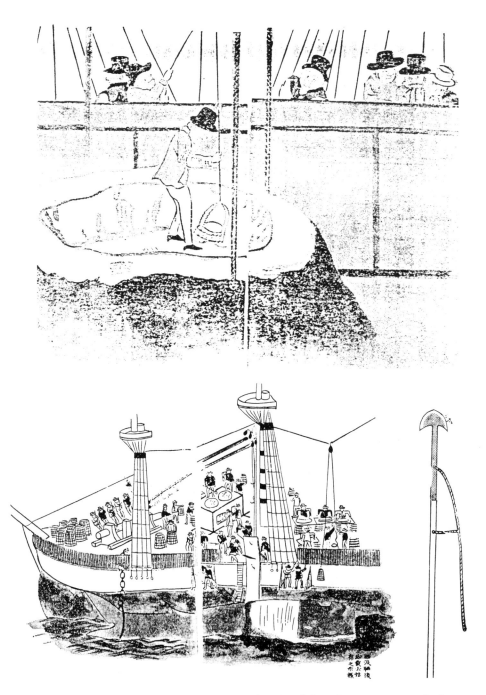

7.   *Bailing spermaceti from the "case" of a sperm whale.
Whaling operations aboard the <u>James Loper</u>. A harpoon.*

8. *The crewman Anthony. Food on the whaler - probably ship's bread and hash or lobscouse. Construction of the crow's nest. The ship's bell.*

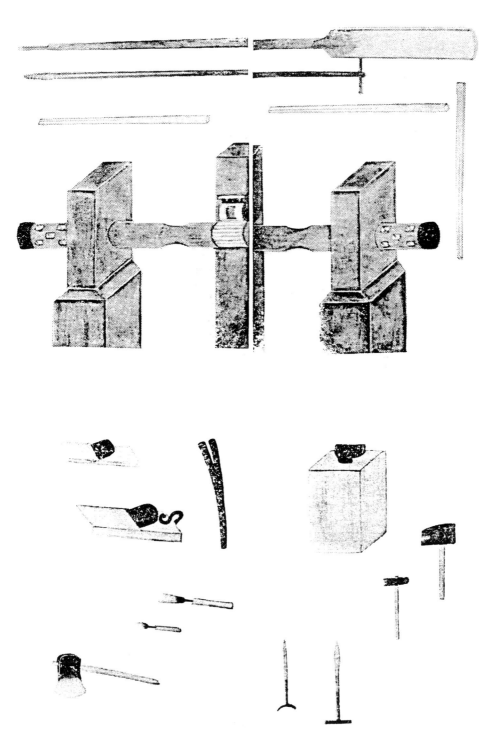

9.   *A windlass for raising anchors, and on whaleships for raising blubber from whales during cutting-in process.*

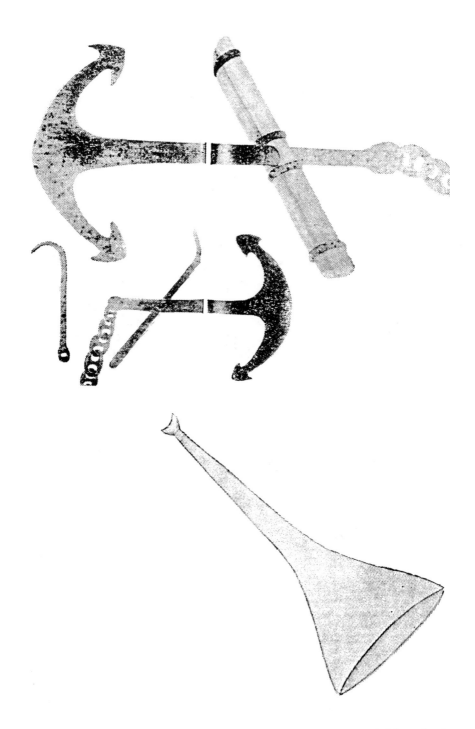

10.   *Anchors, with wooden and iron stocks.   Blubber hook.*
Speaking trumpet.

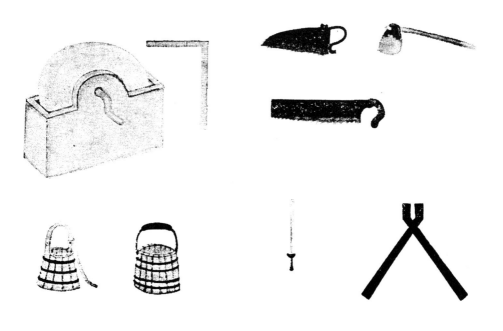

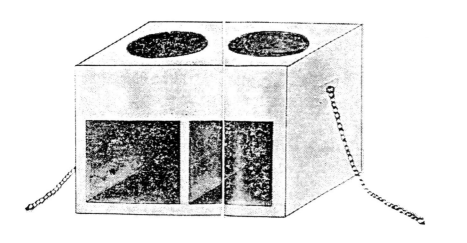

11.   Grindstone for sharpening harpoons, lances, cutting
spades. Tryworks for rendering oil from blubber.

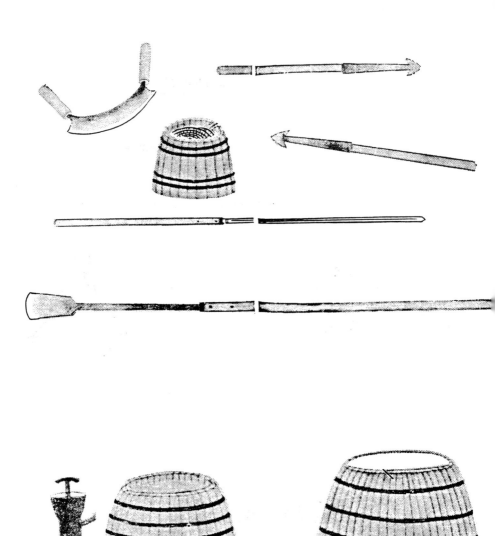

12. *Mincing knife for scoring blubber before trying out.*
Harpoons. A line tub for storing harpoon line. Boarding
knife for severing large pieces of blubber. Cutting spade
for cutting-in whales. Pump. Casks for whale oil.

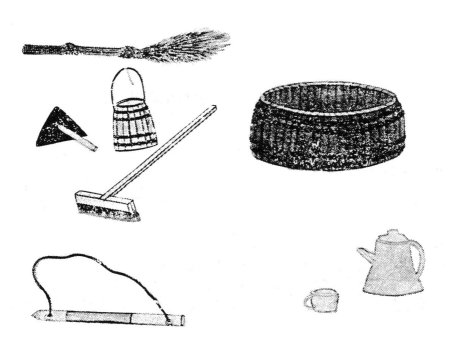

13.   *A cooling vat, for cooling oil before storage in casks.*
      Deck scrubbing equipment.

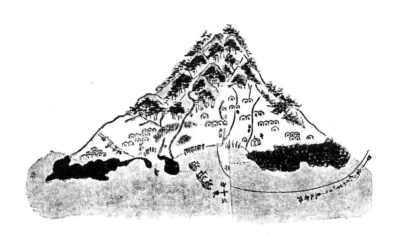

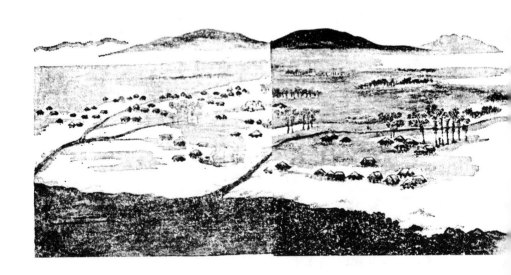

14.   *Wailuku port on Maui Island.   Wailuku beach area,
showing the local magistrate's house, church, ntavie huts,
and sugar press.*

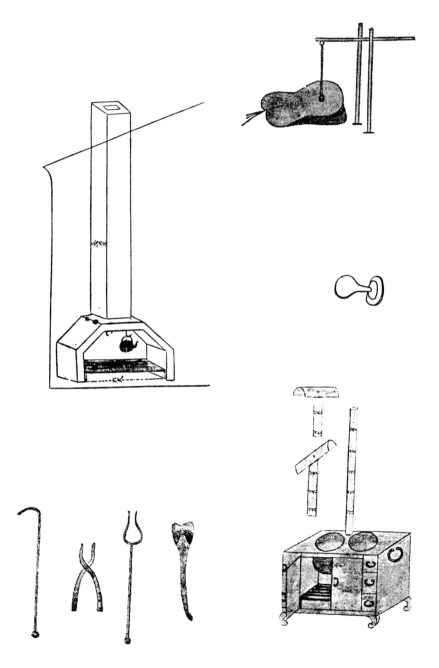

15.   *Furnishings in Rev. Baldwin's house, Lahaina; fireplace; bellows; doorknob; cooking implements (length, left & right 2', 1', 2', 1.5"); and range.*

16.   *Hawaii Island: Hilo harbor and volcano. The residence
of the Chinese in Hilo.*

17.   *Mauna Loa volcano from Hilo. Arrival at Honolulu.*

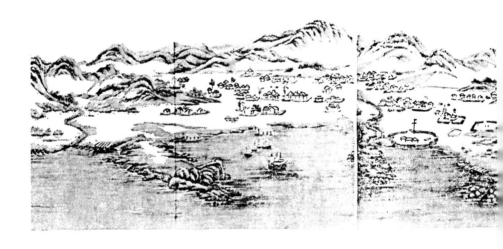

18. *Two views of Oahu harbor at Honolulu: the King's Palace may be seen on the right, in enclosure; Rev. Bingham's house; four churches in one area, two piers, three breakwaters, a salt manufacturing place, the slaughtering hut (near breakwater on the left), and the homes of the butchers and slaughterers.*

19. *Rev. Bingham. Rev. and Mrs. Bingham going to church.*
Captin Heishiro's grave marker; flowers of the plant that
Rev. Bingham planted on the grave; and the fence around
the grave.

20.   King Hamehameha III and the view from the Palace. The
flag and the Palace grounds.

21.   *Native men and women on Oahu Island.*

22.   *A Bengali man; a Frenchman; a Spaniard; and a Black man, playing the fiddle.*

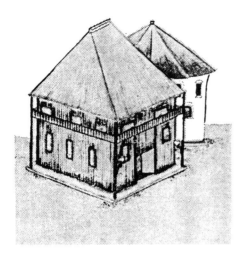

23.   *American's residences. Harbor entrance (on the right), the*
morning marketplace, and huts for natives and servants.

24.   *Papiyo, dressed to go out, and at home. His store.*

25.   *Papiyo's house; and entrance. A Cantonese with a watch.
        A lantern, showing the spring device.*

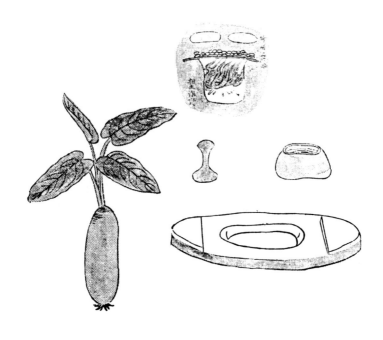

26.   *Taro, and utensils for making poi. A vendor selling poi.*

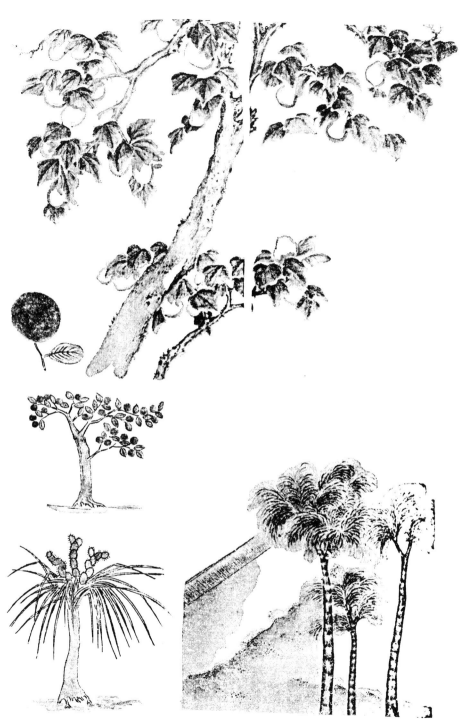

27.   *A cotton plant. Breadfruit and tree; <u>maina</u> (cotton).*

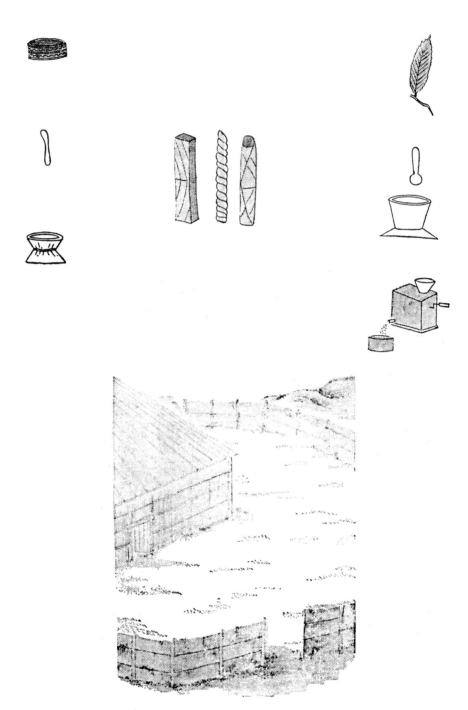

28. *A tobacco case; mortar and pestle for grinding tobacco; rolled tobacco. Pepperberries and leaf. A cattle pen on a ranch.*

29.   *Taking a cow to the slaughterhouse.*

30.   *The slaughterhouse and the storehouse for hides, showing hides drying on the beach. Right: the slaughterhouse, showing cow tied up outside. The carcass ahnging from a beam, and a diagram of the floor, showing the openings for the blood to flow through to the sea.*

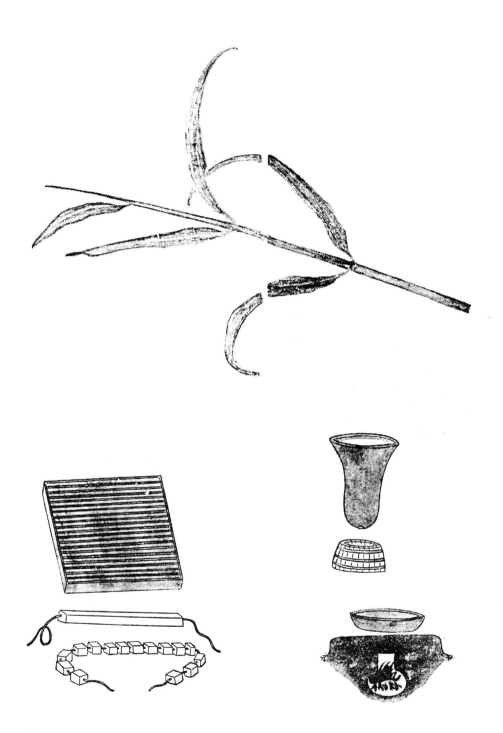

*31.   Sugar manufacturing: a sprig of sugar cane. Implements
for making rock sugar. Cauldron for boiling the juice.*

32.   *Sugar manufacturing.*

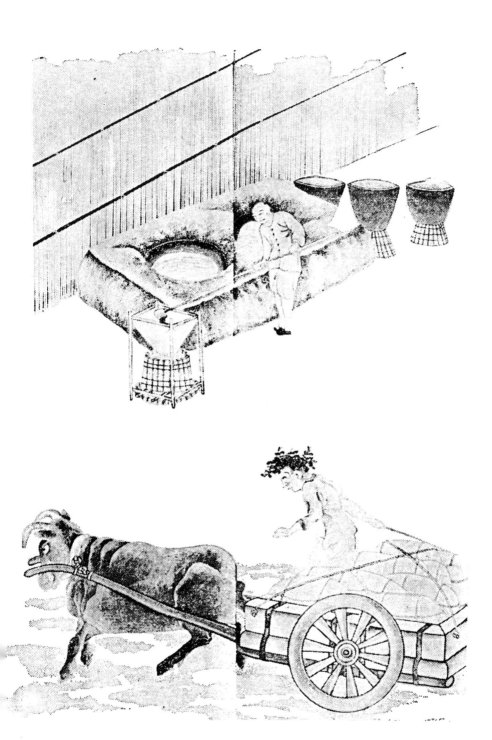

33.	*Sugar manufacturing:	The stone troughs and funnel-
shaped posts. Transporting the sugar.*

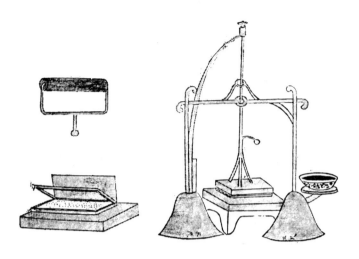

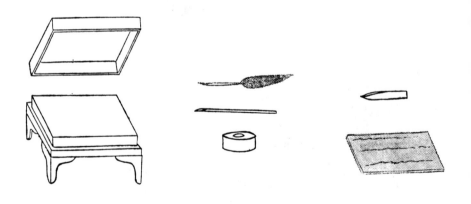

34.   *Printing. The printing press, showing the roller for applying the ink. The stone place for making engravings; the cover and stand are of wood. Pens and ink. A slate and writing implement.*

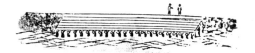

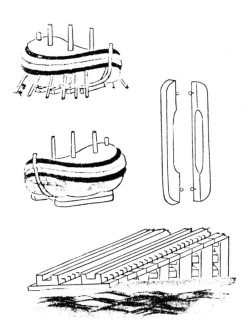

35.   *Ship repair facilities: the slip in Honolulu; T-shaped
      loading dock.*

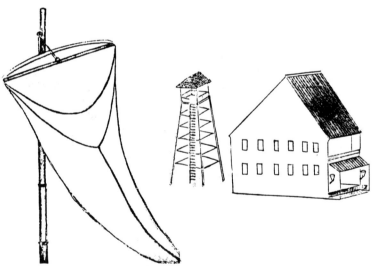

36. *A missionary school, Oahu, with cooling device attached to the exterior, consisting of a cotton sail and wooden pole. When the wood blew through the bag it wade it cool. Also used on ships. A close-up of the cooling device. A cooling shelf beside the house, 11 meters high and 3 meters square.*

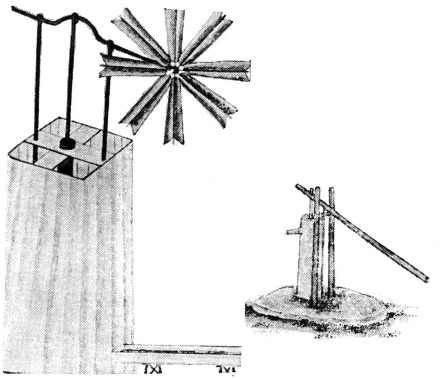

37.   *Windmill and pump.   On left side of the roof of the building a "cooling shelf."*

38.   *Salt manufacturing implements and sacks. The salt beach on Lanai Island.*

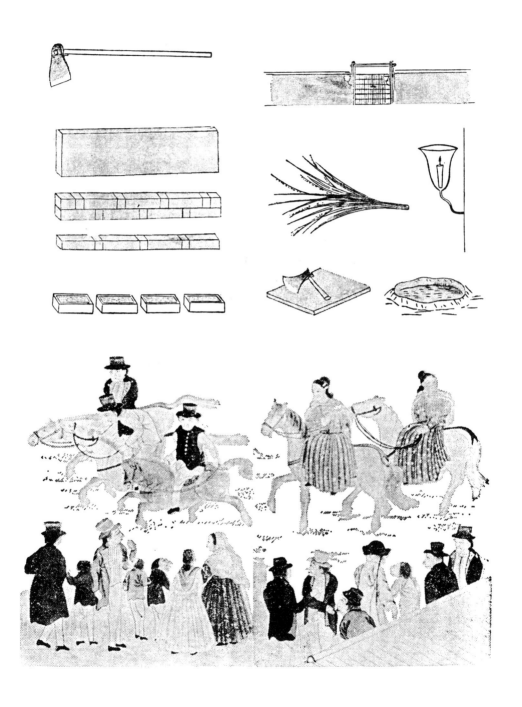

39.   *Preparations for making an adobe wall. Men and women riding bareback.*

40. *Catching a wild boar. Horse with saddle. Riding a tortoise.*

41.   *Rev. Bingham's leavetaking on the <u>Flora</u>.*

42.   *Captains Sen and Carter. Sleeping quarters aboard ship.*

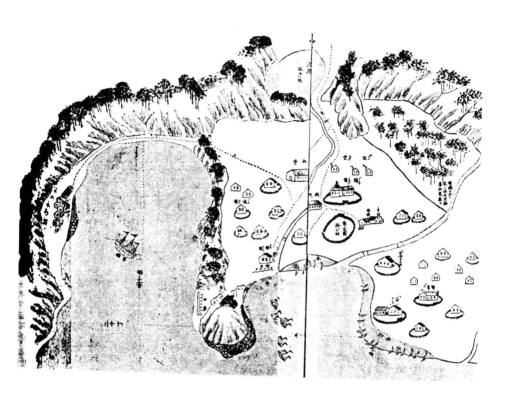

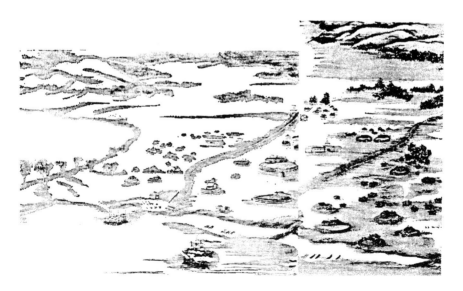

43.   *Petropavlovsk. Kamchatka Harbor.*

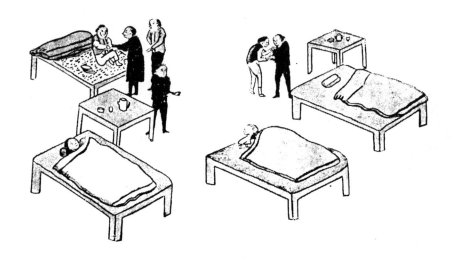

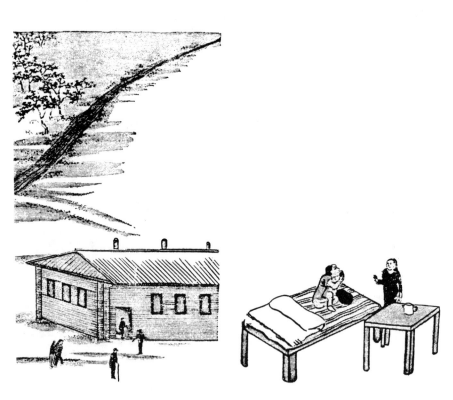

44.   *The hospital at Petropavlovsk.*

45.   *Kamchatka house; dogs chained up; going for firewood.*

46.   *Petropavlovsk society.*

47.   *A wedding. Measuring a man's height.*

48. *The flogging of a male nurse (from <u>Tokei Monogatari</u>).*
Winter sports.

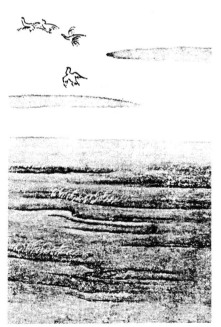

49.   *Hunting scenes.*

50.   *A Petropavlovsk dwelling. Killing a goat.*

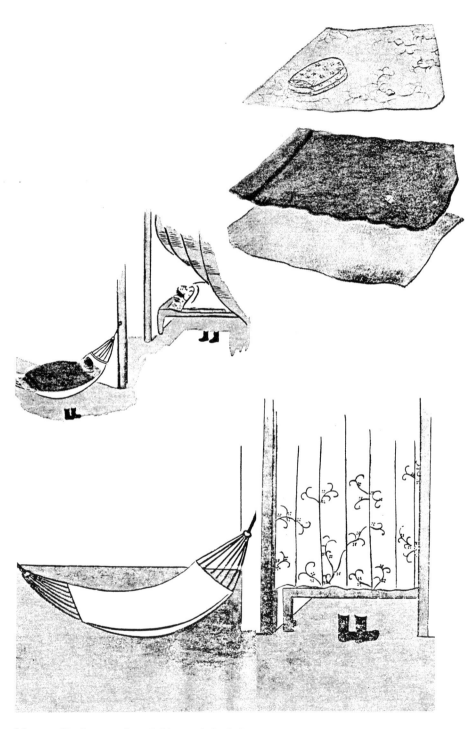

51.   *Bedroom furnishings (cloth hanging in doorway).*

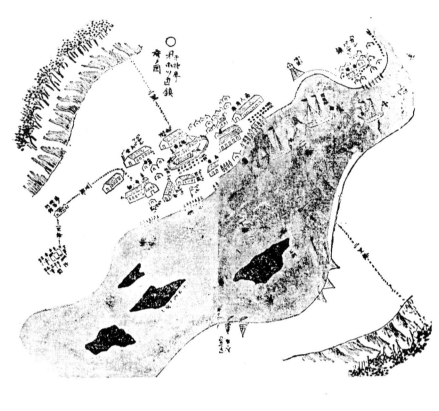

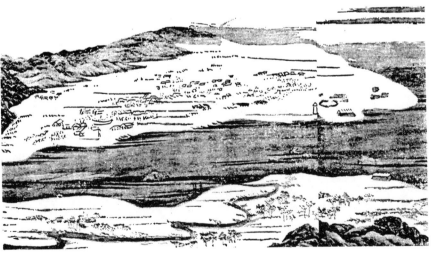

52.   *Okhotsk settlement and harbor.*

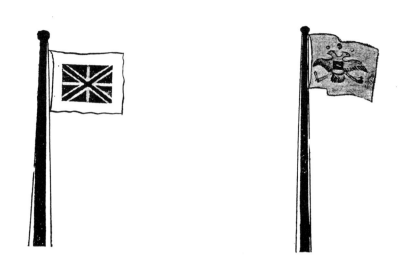

53.   *Commandant's house.   On right, flag of the Russian-American Company.*

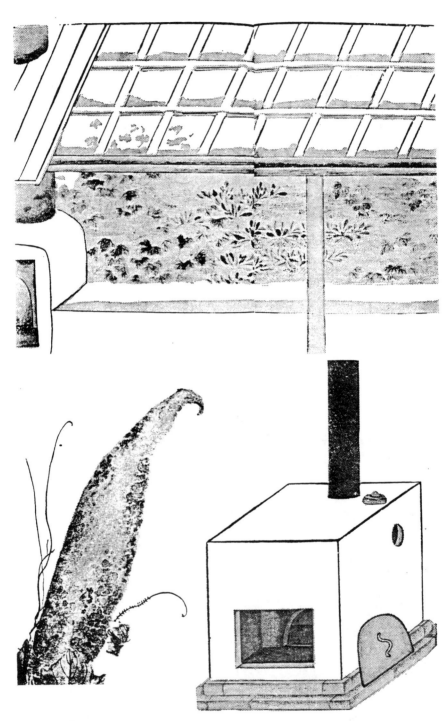

54.   *Hothouse. Plant. Stove.*

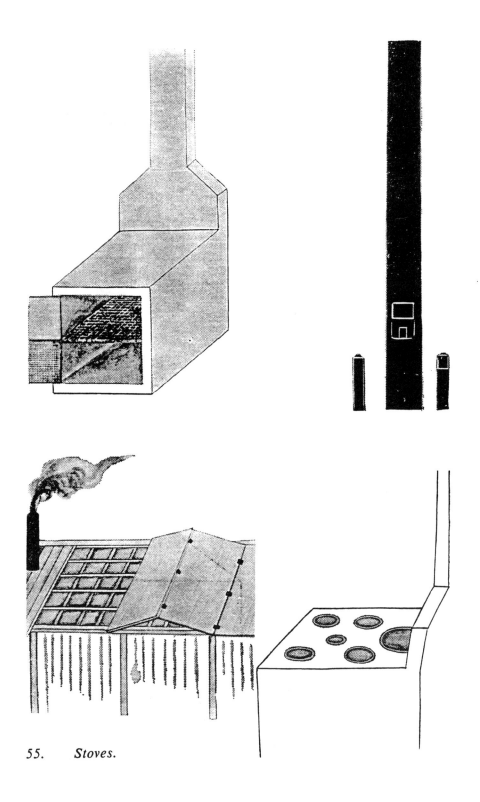

55. *Stoves.*

56. *Commandant, at home and in uniform. Commandant's daughter, showing types of hair arrangements.*

57.   *Feminine styles.*

58.   *Feminine styles.*

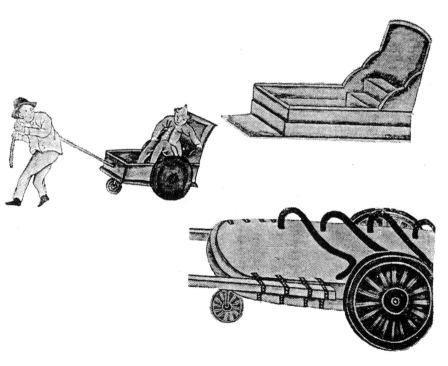

59.   *Transport.*

60.   *Tungus people. Dog. Street Scene.*

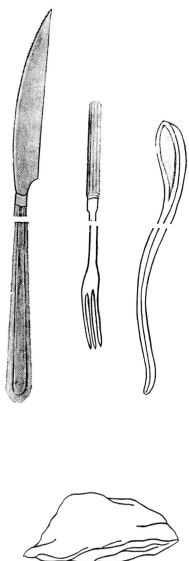

61.   *Eating utensils. Towel or napkin.*

62.   *Soldier receiving beating.   Fettered malefactor at work.*
Another, with nose cut off.

63.   *Troops and weapons.*

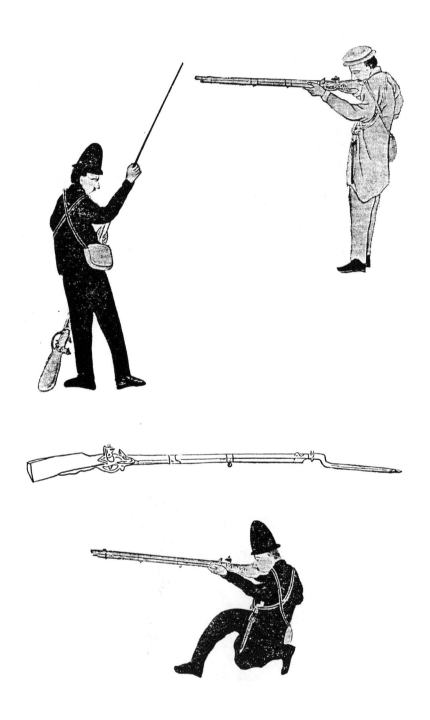

64.　Troops and weapons.

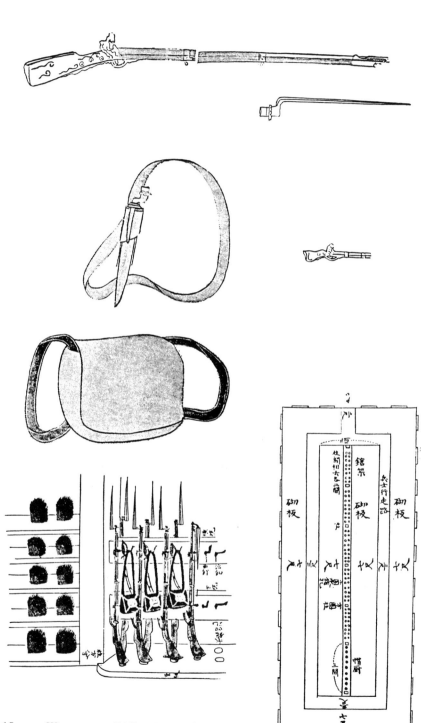

65.   Weapons. Rifles in rack.

66.   *Countryside near Okhotsk.   Commandant and wife on
       journey.*

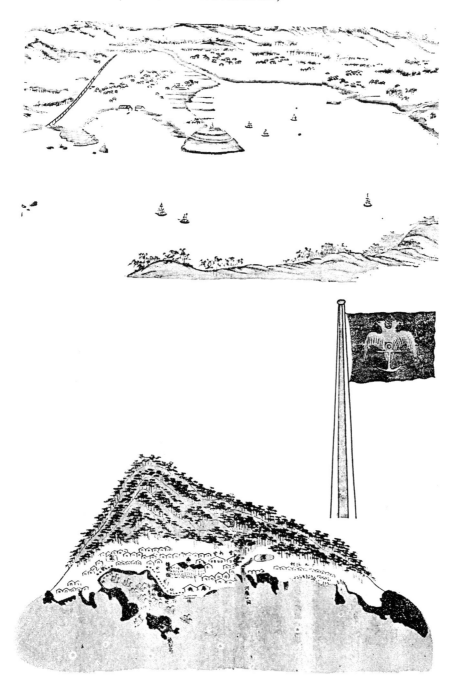

67.   *Sitka: town and port. Russian-American Company flag.*

68.   *The governor's castle.   The governor.   Guard.   Drifters in new clothes.*

69. *Sitka inhabitants: A Russian, and three Kolosh (Tlingit), one with a deer carcass.*

70.   *The Russian steam bath.*

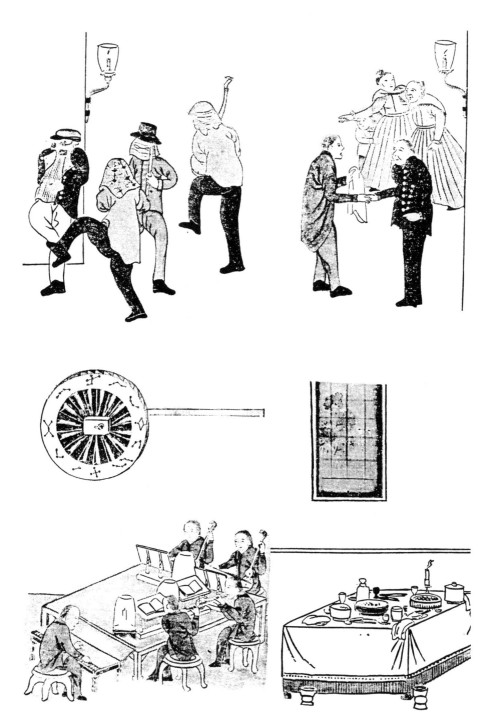

71.   *At the governor's party; masqueraders.   Banquet table.*
Musicians.

72.   *The governor's party, cont'd.*

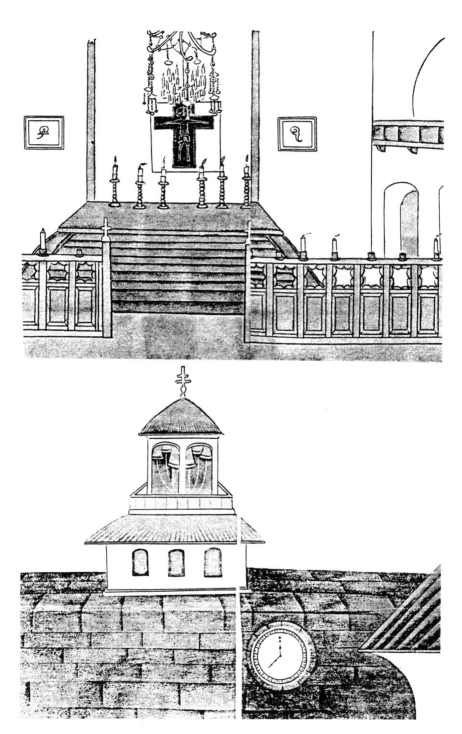

73.   The church.

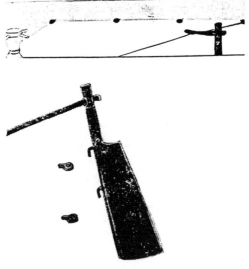

74.   *The Russian steamship (<u>Nikolai I</u>).*

75. *Equipment; two-hatch and three-hatch baidarkas.*

76.   *At the castle: Servant announces arrival of the drifters.*

77.   *Presentation of the clock.*

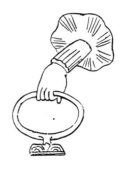

78.   *The clock; infant in cradle; "bottle" for infant.*

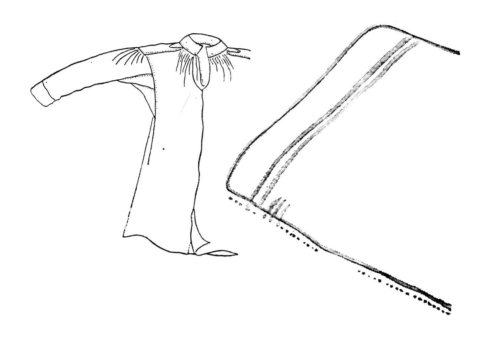

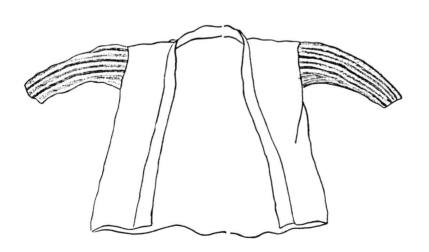

79-85. *Items of daily use.*

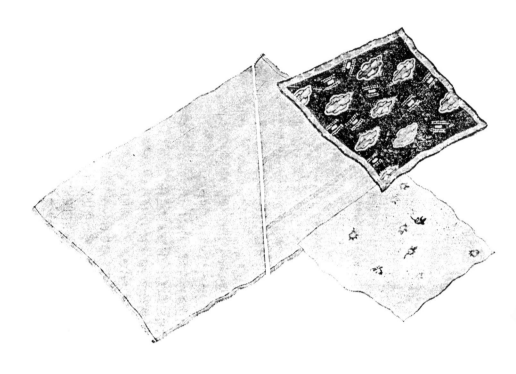

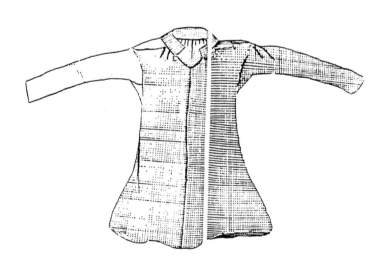

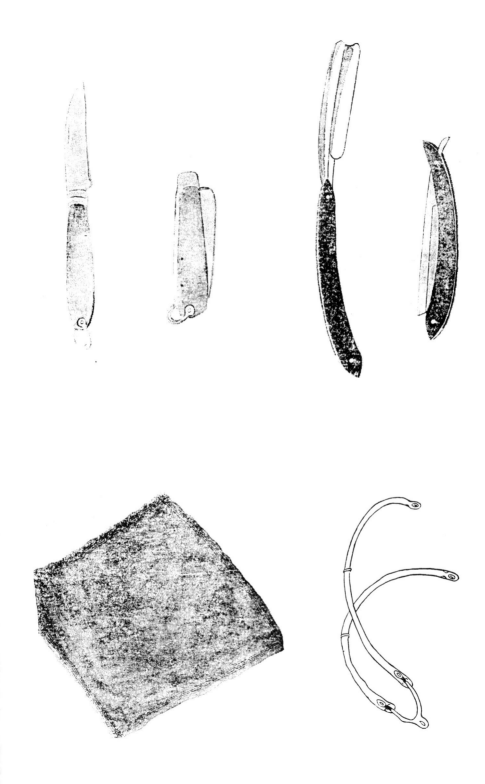

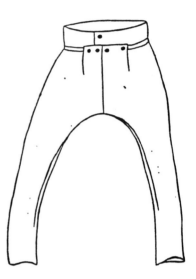

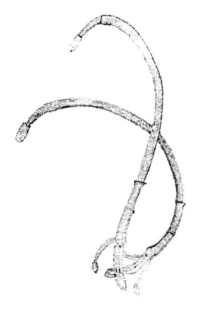

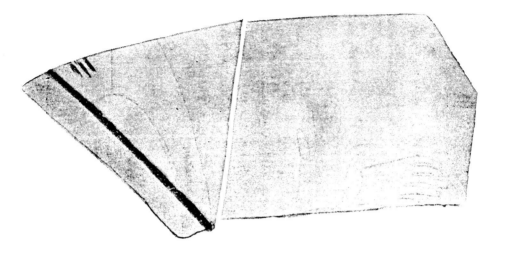

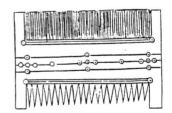

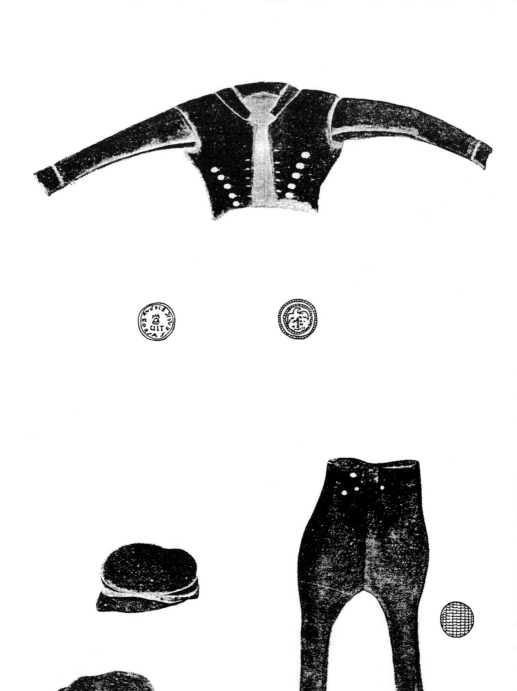

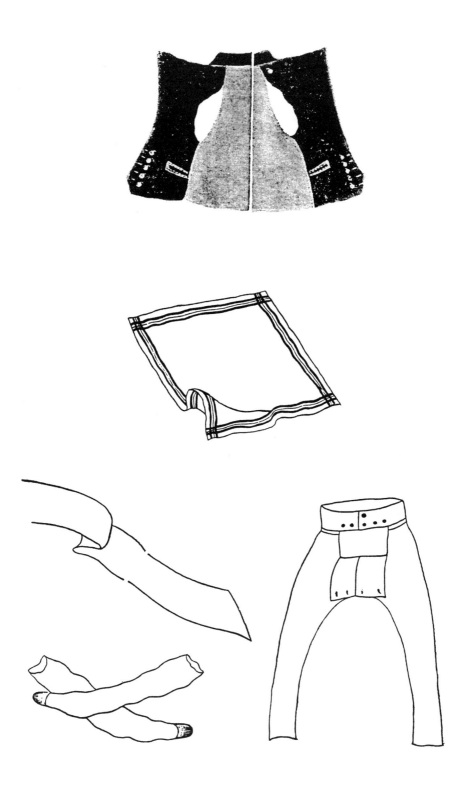

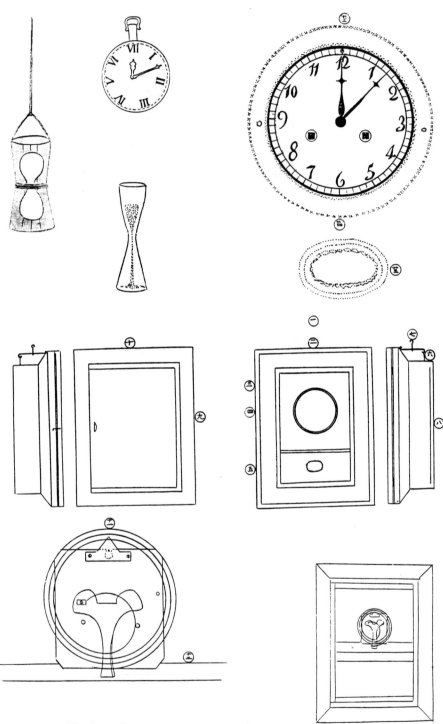

86-87. Clockwork.

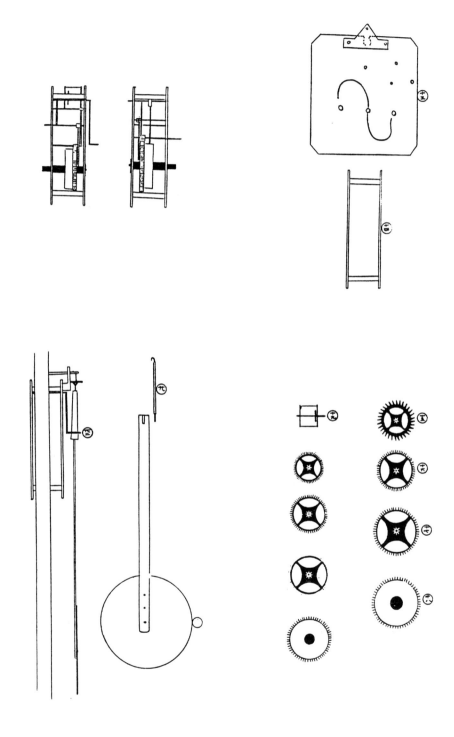

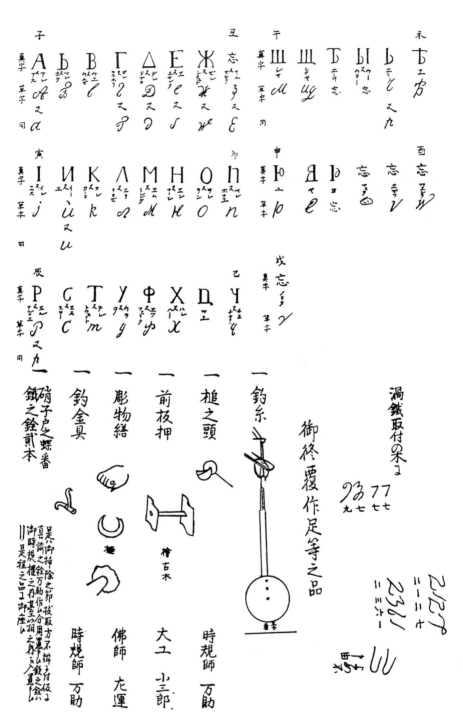

88. *The Russian alphabet, miscellaneous.*

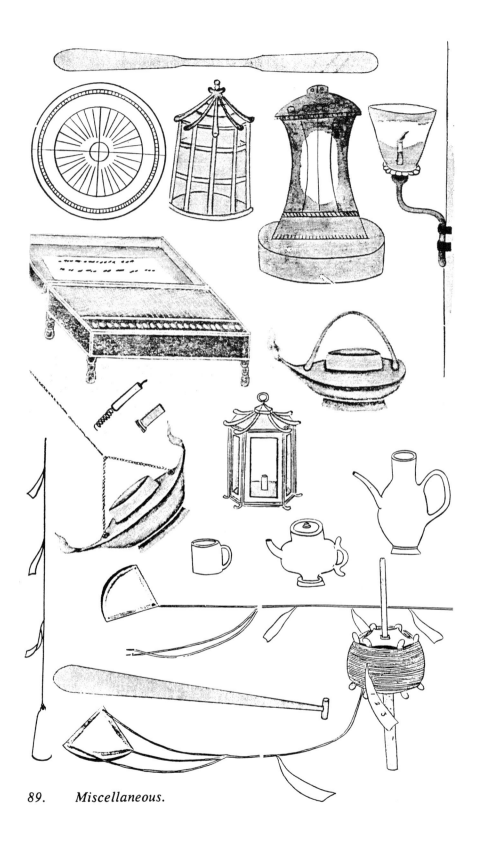

89. *Miscellaneous.*

90. *Etorofu Island.*

THE LIMESTONE PRESS

ALASKA HISTORY SERIES

1. R.A. Pierce, ALASKAN SHIPPING, 1867-1878. ARRIVALS AND DEPARTURES AT THE PORT OF SITKA. 1972. 72 pp., illus. Shipping at the end of the Russian regime and during the first decade of American rule.

2. F.W. Howay. A LIST OF TRADING VESSELS IN THE MARITIME FUR TRADE, 1785-1825. 1973. 209 pp., bibliog., index. Fundamental work on early Northwest Coast

3. K.T. Khlebnikov. LIFE OF BARANOV. 1973. 140 pp., illus., index. Biog. of the first governor of the Russian colonies in America. Tr. from Russ. ed. of 1835   OUT OF PRINT

4. S.G. Fedorova. THE RUSSIAN POPULATION IN ALASKA AND CALIFORNIA, LATE 18TH CENTURY TO 1867. 1973. 367 pp., illus., maps, index. Tr. From Russ. ed. of 1971.

5. V.N. Berkh. A CHRONOLOGICAL HISTORY OF THE DISCOVERY OF THE ALEUTIAN ISLANDS. 1974. 121 pp., illus., maps, index. Tr. of Russ. ed. of 1823   OUT OF PRINT

6. R. V. Makarova. RUSSIANS ON THE PACIFIC, 1743-1799. 1975 301 pp., illus., maps, index. Tr. from Russ. ed. of 1968.   OUT OF PRINT

7. DOCUMENTS ON THE HISTORY OF THE RUSSIAN-AMERICAN COMPANY. 1976. 220 pp., illus., maps, index Tr. from Russ. ed. of 1957

8. R.A. Pierce. RUSSIA'S HAWAIIAN ADVENTURE, 1815-1817. 1976. 245 pp., illus., maps, index. Reprint of 1965 ed..

9. H. W. Elliott. THE SEAL ISLANDS OF ALASKA. Reprint of the 1881 edition, prepared for the Tenth Census of the United States. 176 pp., large format, many illus., Fundamental work on Alaska sealing and the Pribilof Islands.

10. G.I. Davydov. TWO VOYAGES TO RUSSIAN AMERICA, 1802-1807. 1977. 257 pp., illus., maps, index. Transl. from the Russ edition of 1810-1812. Lively account of travel, history and ethnography in Siberia and Alaska.

11. THE RUSSIAN ORTHODOX RELIGIOUS MISSION IN AMERICA, 1794-1807. 1977. 257 pp., illus., index. 186 pp. Transl. of the Russ. edition of 1894. Documents on the mission and the life of its most famous member, the monk German (St. Herman), with ethnographic notes on the Kodiak islanders and Aleuts by the hiermonk Gedeon.   OUT OF PRINT

12. H.M.S. SULPHUR ON THE NORTHWEST AND CALIFORNIA COASTS, 1837 AND 1839. Accounts by Capt. Edward Belcher and Midshipman G. Simpkinson, concerning native peoples of Russian America and California. 1979. 144 pp., illus., maps.

13. P.A. Tikhmenev. A HISTORY OF THE RUSSIAN-AMERICAN COMPANY. Vol. 2: DOCUMENTS. Appendices to a classic account. (Vol. 1 publ. by U. of Washington Press, 1978), Transl. from the Russ. edition of 1861-1863.

14. N.A. Ivashintsov. RUSSIAN ROUND-THE-WORLD VOYAGES, 1803-1849. 1980. 156 pp., illus., maps. Transl. from Russ. ed. of 1849, with supplementary list of voyages to 1867. Summaries, based on logs, indicating ports of call, activities and personnel. Essential for several fields of research. Illus.

15. Wrangell, Baron Ferdinand von. RUSSIAN AMERICA. STATISTICAL AND ETHNOGRAPHIC INFORMATION ON THE RUSSIAN POSSESSIONS ON THE NORTHWEST COAST OF AMERICA. Tr from the German edition, publ. in St. P., 1839. 1980. 204 pp.

16. THE JOURNAL OF IAKOV NETSVETOV: THE ATKA YEARS, 1828-1844. Transl. by Lydia Black from the unpubl. manuscript, with notes and supplements on the history and ethnography of the Aleutian Islands. 1980. 340 pp.,

17. SIBERIA AND NORTHWESTERN AMERICA, 1788-1792. THE JOURNAL OF CARL HEINRICH MERCK, NATURALIST WITH THE RUSSIAN SCIENTIFIC EXPEDITION LED BY CAPTAIN JOSEPH BILLINGS AND GAVRILL SARYCHEV. Tr. by Fritz Jaenach from the unpub. Ger. manuscript. Includes ethnographic, biological and geological observations. Illus., maps, index, 1980

18. David Hunter Miller. THE ALASKA TREATY. 1981. 221 pp., Definitive study of the Alaska purchase, prepared in 1944 for the U.S. Dept. of State's Treaty Series, but never published.

19. G.I. Shelikhov. **VOYAGE TO AMERICA, 1783-1785.** 1981. 162 pp., illus., maps, index, supplementary materials. Tr. from Russ. ed. of 1812. Includes Shelikhov's book, publ. in 1791, with materials erroneously attributed to him since early 19th century.

20. **KODIAK AND AFOGNAK LIFE, 1868-1870.** The Journals of Lts. E.L. Huggins and John Campbell, and merchant Frederick Sargent, with other materials relating to the first years of the American regime in Alaska, including portraits, and early map of Kodiak. Details on ship movements, personnel, trade and life style. 1981. 163 pp.

21. M.D. Teben'kov. **ATLAS OF THE NORTHWEST COASTS OF AMERICA FROM BERING STRAIT TO CAPE CORRIENTES AND THE ALEUTIAN ISLANDS WITH SEVERAL SHEETS ON THE NORTHEAST COAST OF ASIA.** Compiled by Teben'kov while governor of Russian America, and publ. in 1852. 39 sheets, boxed, with softbound vol. with rare **HYDROGRAPHIC NOTES** (109 pp.) and supplementary information. 1981.

22. G.R. Adams. **LIFE ON THE YUKON, 1865-1867.** 1982. 219 pp., illus. From ms. diary of a participant in the Western Union Telegraph Expedition, and his autobiographical account, written later.

23. Dorothy Jean Ray. **ETHNOHISTORY IN THE ARCTIC: THE BERING STRAIT ESKIMO.** Articles, assembled in one volume for the first time, on early trade, the legendary 17th century Russian settlement, the history of St. Michael, Eskimo picture writing, land tenure and polity, settlement and subsistence patterns, and place names. Transl. of Russ. accounts of the Vasil'ev-Shishmarev expedition (1819-1822). 280 pp., illus., maps.

24. Lydia Black. **ATKA. AN ETHNOHISTORY OF THE WESTERN ALEUTIANS.** 1984. 219 pp., illus. Problems of prehistory, ethnography, and 18th century foreign contacts, with a list of Russian voyages, the account of navigator Vasil'ev (1811-1812), Fr. Ioann Veniaminov, and biographical materials.

25. **THE RUSSIAN-AMERICAN COMPANY. CORRESPONDENCE OF THE GOVERNORS. COMMUNICATIONS SENT: 1818.** 1984. xiv, 194 pp., illus., index, notes. Transl. of seldom-used manuscript material in U.S. National Archives.

26. . **THE JOURNALS OF IAKOV NETSVETOV: THE YUKON YEARS, 1845-1863.** 1984. 505 pp., illus., maps. Tr. by Lydia Black from unpub. ms. in Library of Congress, with notes and appendices on the history and ethnography of the Yukon and Kuskokwim regions of Alaska.

27. Ioann Veniaminov. (St. Innokentii). **NOTES ON THE ISLANDS OF THE UNALASHKA DISTRICT.** 1985. 511 pp., illus. Tr. from Russ. ed., St. P., 1840. A classic account.

28. R.A. Pierce. **BUILDERS OF ALASKA: THE RUSSIAN GOVERNORS, 1818-1867.** Biographies of Alaska's 13 forgotten governors, from Hagemeister to Maksutov. 1986. 53 pp., illus.

29. Frederic Litke: **A VOYAGE AROUND THE WORLD, 1826-1829.** Vol. I: TO RUSSIAN AMERICA AND SIBERIA, 1839-1849. Tr. from French ed. (Paris, 1835) by R. Marshall; with a parallel account by F.H. Baron von Kittlitz, tr. from the German ed of 1854 by V.J. Moessner. 1987. 232 pp., maps, illus.

30. A.I. Alekseev. **THE ODYSSEY OF A RUSSIAN SCIENTIST: I.G. VOZNESENSKII IN ALASKA, CALIFORNIA AND SIBERIA, 1839-1849.** Tr. from he Russ. ed. (Moscow, 1977), by Wilma C. Follette. Edited by R.A. Pierce. 1988. 130 pp., illus., maps.

31. Ann Fienup-Riordan, ed. **THE YUP'IK ESKIMO AS DESCRIBED IN THE TRAVEL JOURNALS AND ETHNOGRAPHIC ACCOUNTS OF JOHN AND EDITH KILBUCK, 1885-1900.** 1988. lvii + 528 pp., illus., maps.

32. **THE ROUND THE WORLD VOYAGE OF HIEROMONK GIDEON, 1803-1809.** Tr. with intro. and notes by Lydia T. Black. 1989. xiii + 184 pp., illus., maps.

33. R.A. Pierce. **RUSSIAN AMERICA: A BIOGRAPHICAL DICTIONARY.** 1990. xxii + 570 pp.

34. A.I. Alekseev. **THE DESTINY OF RUSSIAN AMERICA.** Tr. from the Russian ed. of 1975. 1990.

35. **RUSSIA IN NORTH AMERICA. PROCEEDINGS OF THE 2D INTERNATIONAL CONFERENCE ON RUSSIAN AMERICA.** Sitka, Alaska, August 19-22, 1987. 1990.

SEA OF OKHOTSK

Bol'sheretsk

KAMCHATKA

Nizhne-Kamchatsk

Karaginskii I.

Bering I.
KOMANDORSKIE I.
Mednyi I.
(Copper) I.

BERING

SEA

NEAR I. Attu
Agattu I.

St. Ma

Kiska I.
RAT I. Amchitka I.
PRIB

Tanaga I. ALEUTIAN
Adak I.
ANDREIANOV I.

Atkha I.
ISLAN

ISLANDS OF
THE FOUR
MOUNTAINS

Siberia

RUSSIAN
AMERICA

Okhotsk

CHINA

Sitka

JAPAN

Ft.Ross
San Francisco

UNITED
STATES

Sandwich I.

PHILIPPINE I.

MEXICO

NORTH PACIFIC AREA 1818